FROM

Correcting **101** Common Bowling Errors

GUTTERBALLS TO STRIKES

Mike Durbin with Dan Herbst

CB

CONTEMPORARY BOOKS

Library of Congress Cataloging-in-Publication Data

Durbin, Mike.
    From gutterballs to strikes : correcting 101 common bowling errors / Mike
Durbin with Dan Herbst.
        p.   cm.
    Includes index.
    ISBN 0-8092-3058-5
    1. Bowling.   I. Herbst, Dan.   II. Title.
GV903.D87   1997
794.6—dc21   97-24595
                                                                       CIP

Cover design by Todd Petersen
Cover and interior photographs by Russ Vitale
Interior design by Nick Panos

Published by Contemporary Books
A division of NTC/Contemporary Publishing Group, Inc.
4255 West Touhy Avenue, Lincolnwood (Chicago), Illinois 60712-1975 U.S.A.
Copyright © 1998 by Dan Herbst
All rights reserved. No part of this book may be reproduced, stored in a retrieval
system, or transmitted in any form or by any means, electronic, mechanical,
photocopying, recording, or otherwise, without the prior written permission of
NTC/Contemporary Publishing Group, Inc.
Printed in the United States of America
International Standard Book Number: 0-8092-3058-5

02 03 04 05 ML 20 19 18 17 16 15 14 13 12 11 10 9 8 7 6 5

Mike Durbin: This book is dedicated to my wife, Debbie, for 33 years of love, support, encouragement, and advice. A special thanks to my most loyal fan, who first introduced me to bowling—my dad, Bill Durbin, who passed away in 1991. I will always be grateful to my mother, Pat Durbin, for passing on her determination and perseverance. A special mention to three great children—Mike, Jr., Chrissie, and Matt.

Dan Herbst: I wish to dedicate my efforts to Sandy Herbst for giving 10 great years of love, friendship, partnership, and patience.

Contents

Introduction		vii
Chapter 1	The Pre-Shot Routine	1
Chapter 2	Timing	15
Chapter 3	The Armswing	25
Chapter 4	The Release	39
Chapter 5	The Finish	57
Chapter 6	Physical Adjustments	67
Chapter 7	Equipment	83
Chapter 8	Converting Spares and Splits	105
Chapter 9	Practice	121
Chapter 10	The Mental Game	135
Appendix	101 Common Bowling Errors	159
Index		163

Introduction

A lot of great things have happened to me in the three decades since I left home to try my luck on the Professional Bowlers Association's National Tour. I've matched my skills and wits against the greatest bowlers in the world. Since 1980, I have covered the championship round of tournaments from New York to California for ESPN. And I have served as the manager of one of America's most prominent bowling centers.

My career has exceeded my wildest expectations. From being selected as the Professional Bowlers Association's (PBA) Rookie of the Year in 1967 to becoming the only player to win the Firestone Tournament of Champions three times, I have been fortunate. I won 14 times on the National Tour and was inducted into the PBA Hall of Fame.

These are all great memories. But as far as I'm concerned, the best reward was simply being able to do for a living what I love to do the most. While crisscrossing this fantastic country, I met so many sincere and nice people, from my fellow competitors to PBA sponsors to the most loyal fans in all of sports. I know that I have truly been blessed.

For me, bowling is not only a highly competitive sport, it's my job. For most people, however, it's a superb form of recreation. Like anything we do in life, it gives us even more pleasure when we do it well. It's my hope that this book will help you knock over more pins and, with that, gain a greater enjoyment from your trips to the lanes.

One of my roles with ESPN is "Mr. Average Builder." In that capacity I've presented countless pointers to viewers on how to bowl better. Because of that series, Contemporary Books asked me to take on a new role, that of an author. It was their feeling that my experience bowling with and observing thousands of amateurs during PBA Pro-Am events would provide me with insight as to the shortcomings that prevent many from achieving higher scores.

Most instructional books tell you what to do. That's fine. But knowing how to correct mistakes is a very big part of any athletic endeavor. That's why coaches serve such a vital role. With the exception of top-level players, few bowlers have the benefit of personal coaching. Thus, most players must be able to both recognize and correct their own mistakes. By learning 101 of the most common errors, you will improve your game dramatically.

I have attempted to break down the delivery into its various components to help you learn your own game and coach yourself to great matches. In addition, on pages 156-157 you'll find a handy chart to help you recognize and fix 10 prominent errors. Feel free to copy it and slip it into your bowling bag for reference.

Of all the advice you'll find in this book, the most important tip I can provide is to remind you that bowling—even on the professional level—ought to be fun. The more positive your attitude, the more enjoyment you'll get out of the game. And the more you enjoy bowling, the better you will bowl. It's no accident that the greatest players in the history of bowling are people who genuinely love to bowl.

CHAPTER 1

The Pre-Shot Routine

I n a sport in which the ability to repeat a series of movements is a key ingredient of success, forming good habits is essential. Virtually all professional bowlers have a pre-shot routine. What may seem like a series of superstitions to the casual observer is, in fact, a set series of actions that gives the athlete a physical and psychological edge.

The former relates to automatically undergoing a de facto checklist. For example, by always wiping your ball with a towel before inserting your fingers into the holes, you remove any lane dressing (oil used to condition the bowling lane) that was transferred from the alley to your ball. Doing so prevents oil from accumulating on your ball, which, if allowed to build up, could alter the way your shots react.

Preparing for every delivery in the same manner can help you relax and focus. Your actions prior to the most important shot of a competition should be exactly the same as when rolling a practice shot. That's important because it reminds you that the physical skills to be per-

A comprehensive and consistent pre-shot routine will allow you to achieve your best form more often.

1

formed in a pressure situation aren't any different than those you've performed successfully countless times before.

Before every frame, make certain that the ball is free of oil and other foreign substances.

MISTAKE 1

Not Having a Pre-Shot Routine

The failure to adhere to a certain series of actions between stepping onto the approach and releasing the ball is a common shortcoming among amateur bowlers. Like snowflakes, no two routines are identical. However, some important steps should be included in every pre-shot routine, and they will be discussed in this chapter.

MISTAKE 2

Not Checking Your Shoes for Foreign Substances

The danger of neglecting this seemingly trivial detail was driven home to me in the 1970s. At the time I was employed at Bainbridge Colonial Lanes in my hometown of Chagrin Falls, Ohio. Mixing work with pleasure, I was simultaneously working at the bowling center's desk while competing in a classic league. Blame it on the impetuousness of youth, but I must have been determined to prove that one *can* do two things at once.

As with most facilities, our control station was located in the middle of the bowling center. Bainbridge has 24 lanes. Our league was assigned to lanes 17 through 24. I worked with one eye on potential customers and the other on my lane.

As the player ahead of me delivered his strike ball, I walked over to my lane while taking care to step only on dry flooring. That wasn't as easy as it sounds—because Ohio winters include frequent snow, our patrons constantly entered Bainbridge with wet shoes and galoshes. To make matters worse, the flooring was tile rather than carpet.

Each lane had a tiny carpet on the front of the approach that was about the size of a typical bathroom mat. I rubbed my foot on it every time as a precaution, and then I checked my shoe to make sure that no dampness or foreign substance remained that might inhibit my ability to slide with my left (nonbowling) foot.

On most occasions, dodging puddles wasn't that difficult. But once in a while, the need to attend to a customer during my turn required me to sprint so as not to inconvenience my fellow players. And one night I unfortunately discovered the accuracy of the aphorism about haste making waste.

Although I thought I was conscientious about adhering to my routine, I must have unknowingly become so complacent as to neglect it. I reached that conclusion while my body was parallel to the lane!

I had stuck at the line and found myself doing my best Superman imitation as I flew head-first toward the pins. Believe me, a bowling lane isn't to be confused with a trampoline when it comes to landing comfort. That's particularly true when your feet crash five feet on the wrong side of the foul line while your elbows slide pinward on an oiled surface. I'm not sure which hurt more—my body, which ached all over, or my pride.

Even if you aren't constantly running from one end of the bowling center to another when it's your turn to bowl, it's still advisable to check your shoes prior to every frame. Because bowling is such a social sport, you never know what you might step in. Bowling's "sand traps" aren't as readily detectable as those of golf, but they're much more hazardous. They include water, ketchup, beverages, and melted chocolate. Any of these can lead to sticking at the line, which could result in something as minor as missing a spare or, at worst, a serious injury.

Should you discover something on your shoe, it's essential that you clean the bottom of the shoe prior to your delivery. A lot of players use a wire

Cleaning the bottoms of your shoes can save you from both embarrassment and pain.

brush; some use a scouring pad. If neither is available, try a bowling towel.

Assuming that smoking is allowed on the premises, find an ashtray and drop some ashes on the lane's approach. Rub your foot over them and then either use a towel to wipe them away or slide your foot several times on the approach until you are confident that you won't stick at the line.

In some situations, you might have stepped in so much liquid that you just can't get your shoes completely dry. My advice: Spring for a buck and rent alley shoes, but never bowl in footwear that could be hazardous to your health.

MISTAKE 3

Removing the Ball from the Rack Incorrectly

Many bowlers needlessly put their fingers and backs at risk by carelessly removing the bowling ball from the return apparatus. I can understand how the occasional bowler might be ignorant of proper procedure, but league and serious participants should know better.

Don't grab your ball with one hand, and don't lift the ball with your fingers in the holes. Doing so is a great way to get your fingers pinched should another ball hit yours as you are removing it. Another danger is the stress you needlessly place on your wrist and back.

Think of it this way: Would you pick up a bulky package in such a careless manner? And how many packages weigh as much as a bowling ball?

The correct (left) and incorrect (right) way to remove your ball from the rack.

Whether your center has a round-style or straight-line ball-return apparatus, the correct technique for ball removal is the same. First, stand with your legs as close to the ball as possible. Place a hand on each side of your ball with your knees slightly bent. Then, and only then, remove it carefully with both hands.

Don't think that this is an inconsequential habit. Once when I was competing in St. Louis I took a shortcut. The next thing I knew, my finger was smashed. A very uncomfortable blood blister developed under my fingernail, which I had to have lanced between squads. In a sport in which you need your fingers to perform, it's crazy to injure them through negligence.

MISTAKE 4

Incorrect Address Position

Having removed the ball from the rack, you should cradle it in your non-bowling arm. Not only is this a more comfortable method, it also makes it

Cradle the ball in your nonbowling arm as you step onto the approach.

Use the inside edge of your sliding foot to line yourself up prior to assuming the address position.

appear that you actually know what you're doing, even if you don't!

Next, locate your starting mark on the approach. (In Chapter 6, we will cover strategies for lining up.) Regardless of how you are playing the lane, use the inside edge of your sliding foot as a reference point. For example, a right-handed player standing on the 10th board should place the inside of the left foot on that board.

It's common for players to forget where they stood in the previous frame. That never happened to me when I was younger, because I was so focused that no detail escaped my notice. But as I got older, I would sometimes forget. I'm not sure if that's because bowling results are not as important to me as they once were or because of the natural tendency of the aging process to rob one of the ability to pay attention to details over a prolonged period of time.

You can use an air blower (left) or resin bag (right) to dry your bowling hand.

MISTAKE 5

Failing to Dry the Bowling Hand

If you're like me, your palms become sweaty while bowling (the greater the stakes, the greater the perspiration). That's why your pre-shot routine should always include drying your hand. Your options:

1. Use a resin bag.
2. Rub a towel across your bowling hand.
3. Hold your hand over the air blower prior to removing the ball from the rack.

Regardless of which of the above is your preference, before shooting make certain that your hand is bone dry. We have all made enough bad deliveries without needlessly adding to the total by letting a shot slip off the hand due to excess moisture. You won't make a quality shot if the ball slips off your thumb or fingers during your downswing.

By the way, if you like to snack or drink between frames, my suggestion is to only do so with your nonbowling hand.

MISTAKE 6

Taking the Wrong Exit Due to a Poor Entrance

The key to a powerful strike ball is a strong release. Your thumb must exit the ball prior to your fingers so that the middle and ring finger can impart the necessary lift to the shot. A thumb that stays in too long is guaranteed to kill your roll.

As your fingers and thumb enter the ball, the majority of the ball's weight is supported by your nonbowling hand. Believe it or not, the order in which you insert your fingers and thumb into the ball will affect the sequence in which they exit. It is essential that you first put your fingers into their appropriate holes. Only after that is done should you gently lay your relaxed thumb into the ball.

Don't put a death grip on the ball. Many lower-average players squeeze so tightly that their forearms bulge and, in some cases, even their teeth are clenched. You won't execute a smooth release if your muscles are flexed and tense.

MISTAKE 7

Only in Politics Is Being in the Middle an Advantage

A very prevalent pre-shot error is to hold the bowling ball in the center of one's body. This forces your arm to swing circuitously so that the ball goes

A proper armswing isn't possible unless during the address the ball is held in line with your bowling shoulder (as shown at right).

around your hip during the backswing. As we'll soon learn, a straight and unmuscled armswing is far preferable to one that causes the ball to loop.

In the correct address position, the ball is aligned with the shoulder of your bowling arm. It can be held between waist and shoulder height, wherever it feels more comfortable for you, as long as it's in line with that shoulder.

Those who hold the ball in front of the body are almost certain to suffer from what's known as *swingout*, defined as the ball moving away from the body during the backswing. Swingout will force you to make a correction in that swing later in the delivery in order to be accurate.

Some degree of swingout isn't always fatal. Superstars Walter Ray Williams and Dave Husted both had a moderate swingout early in their careers. So did 1970s great Don Johnson. All were able to compensate at the top of the swing to get it back in line.

However—and this is no small consideration—each possessed outstanding athleticism coupled with the advantage of rolling hundreds of

Even a moderate degree of swingout, while not inherently fatal, is undesirable.

That's the case if you have wide hips, so this can be a particularly troublesome area for female players. But whether you're built like a fire hydrant or like a beanpole, don't encourage swingout with a bad starting position.

The ball should rest in the palm of your bowling hand with that hand facing upward. Your fingers are at 6 o'clock. The thumb of a right-handed player is at about 2 o'clock (10 o'clock for left-handed bowlers).

games per week. Both factors made grooving a stroke far less difficult than for someone who rolls but a fraction of that amount.

Even in the pros, avoiding swingout is often a priority. Williams, Husted, and Johnson enjoyed greater success in their careers after straightening their backswings. Hall of Famer Jim Stefanich went so far as to wear a towel-like apparatus under his armpit that forced him to keep his right forearm close to his body during his swing.

Some players may find that a certain degree of swingout is inevitable.

Give some credit to using towels for helping Jim Stefanich wipe up the competition en route to becoming 1968's PBA Player of the Year. *Courtesy of the PBA*

MISTAKE 8

Incorrect Foot Position ✓

I recommend that 60 to 65 percent of your weight be concentrated on the foot opposite your bowling arm. With your knees slightly bent, remain relaxed from head to toe. Just before beginning your delivery, take a deep breath and exhale to further eliminate any tension in your body. I start my pushaway and footwork as I exhale.

Some players stand with their feet parallel to each other (side by side). Others, as recommended by noted coach Fred Borden, keep the opposite foot about six inches closer to the foul line (so that for a right-handed player, the toes of the right foot are lined up with the middle of the left foot). As far as I'm concerned, either technique works just fine, so the one you choose is strictly a matter of personal preference.

I'm a four-step player, so my right hand and right heel move simultaneously. Reminding myself of what I call *synchronized stroking* is one of my mental keys. I try to lift my right heel so that my first step will be definitive, without hesitation. By concentrating the majority of my weight on my opposite foot, I remind myself which foot to begin with.

MISTAKE 9

Failing to Focus on a Target

One of bowling's great debates is whether it's preferable to have accuracy or power. As far as I'm concerned, that's like asking me if I'd rather have a good job or a good family. My answer is that I want both!

One thing is for sure—you won't be accurate if you don't focus on your target. Yet many players fail to establish a specific target.

As a general rule, selecting one of the seven arrows on the lane as a target is your best bet. The manufacturers put them there for just that purpose. They are aligned with the seven visible pins (the 1, 2, 3, 4, 6, 7, and 10 pins).

Many advanced players aim for a specific board (there are 39 boards with five boards separating each arrow). Another tactic is to aim farther down the lane. Better bowlers do this when they wish to get the ball through the head area (the front portion) of the lane and delay the point at which it begins to hook. It's a fairly sophisticated strategy for experienced participants.

Some pros, including former PBA Player of the Year Wayne Webb, use the dots on the foul line as their aiming point. That's a rarely used option, and personally, I find it very disorienting to look straight downward as I release my shot.

To the best of my knowledge, there isn't a single standout player on the men's, women's, or men's senior PBA Tour who aims at the pins. The last great bowler to do that was a three-stepper from California named Lee Jouglard. His career highlight was winning the 1951 American Bowling Congress ABC Masters Tournament. The large number of stars who have come and gone since Jouglard's heyday (and the fact that not one of them pin-bowled) should discourage you from using pins as your aiming point.

Finding a target is a topic in this book's segment on how to best line up your shots (see page 79). What is important is that you always have a target to give you something to line up with and to walk toward.

MISTAKE 10

Failing to Execute a Strong Pushaway

If the start of your delivery is technically correct, it will be much easier for you to repeat the movements that follow. A good pushaway should make your delivery far more consistent.

One rule is that on your pushaway, you want the ball to travel forward the same distance as your initial stride. Push the ball straight ahead toward your target with the majority of its weight still supported by your non-bowling hand as the heel of the right foot (for a right-handed player) hits the ground.

Don't make the common mistake of walking first and then pushing the ball away, or the error of pushing the ball out before your foot moves.

When giving a lesson, I instruct my pupils to visualize a small table in front of the bowling hand. I want them to try to place the ball on that table.

A technically sound pushaway is a key ingredient to obtaining accuracy.

Not every bowler goes by the book with their pushaways. As of this writing, Mike Aulby remains the only player in history to have captured bowling's Grand Slam by having won the ABC Masters Tournament, the U.S. Open, the PBA National Championship, and the Tournament of Champions. Aulby pushes the ball skyward. So, too, did PBA Hall of Famer Tommy Hudson.

Both men compensated for their upward pushaways later in their deliveries. Failure to do so would mean that the sliding foot would precede the ball to the foul line. You can be successful bowling in this manner, but it will be more difficult for you to perform consistently.

Summary

While your pre-shot regimen may vary greatly from mine, the key is consistency in the routine. The following elements should be present in your pre-shot routine.

1. Be physically and psychologically prepared to bowl when it's your turn.
2. Remove the ball correctly from the return apparatus.
3. Make certain that your ball and shoes are completely free of any foreign substances.
4. Check that your bowling hand is dry before inserting your fingers and thumb into the ball.
5. Insert your fingers into the ball prior to your thumb.
6. Find and stand on your optimum starting spot on the approach.
7. The ball is in line with your bowling shoulder during the address position, with the majority of your weight supported by the foot opposite your bowling hand.
8. Focus fully on your target.
9. Relax (a deep breath always helps).
10. Execute a proper pushaway.
11. Be positive: Physically preparing yourself and your equipment for the upcoming delivery is only fruitful if you are confident you're about to make a good shot.

CHAPTER 2

Timing

I t's often said that in life, timing is everything. In bowling, timing is a catch-all phrase that's cited by a lot of people as an excuse for why they performed below expectations on a given occasion. We've all heard one of our bowling buddies complaining, "My timing was off tonight."

Timing is a very convenient target to blame when anything goes awry. This isn't to suggest that poor or inconsistent timing can't be a major culprit. However, more often than not the problem involves your rhythm. That's especially true for above-average players since, with adequate knowledge, timing is a component that can easily be adjusted and corrected.

For the uninitiated, timing refers to the synchronization of the movements of one's feet and bowling arm. Being *in time* is generally defined as the ball reaching the bottom of the armswing (as one is about to release the shot) while the opposite foot is completing its sliding motion. Thus, the right hand and the left foot (right-hander) or

The relationship between armswing and footwork lends credence to the old adage that "timing is everything."

Late (left) and early (right) timing.

the left hand and the right foot (left-hander) arriving simultaneously at the foul line is generally considered to be the ideal.

Some players prefer that the foot slightly precede the hand. By planting, they feel that they gain leverage. That's why many of the sport's power players feature what's referred to as slightly *late* timing. Conversely, the far less prevalent *early* timing occurs when the ball is released before the foot arrives at the foul line.

With all due respect to conventional wisdom, my definition of timing differs from the above. I trust that you'll pardon me for offering my version of the term. I have always considered timing to be the position of my right foot in relation to my right arm at the top of my backswing. (Obviously, a left-handed player's arm and left foot are linked together in the same way.)

It's my opinion that the ball's arrival at the bottom of the swing as the sliding foot gets to the line is related to my finish. The foot-hand relationship at the line is established by what precedes it at the top of the swing. Unless one makes a conscious physical correction on the downswing that involves the undesirable technique of employing muscle rather than gravity to pull the arm downward, the foot-hand relationship during your release will be the same as it was at the top of your armswing.

By my definition, being in time means the ball arrives at the peak of your backswing at the exact instant that the same-side foot is flat on the floor during your next-to-last step. Thus, the right foot and right hand of a right-handed player (and vice versa for a lefty) are in sync. This applies whether you feature an abbreviated back-swing like Roy Buckley's in which the ball only reaches waist height, or an ultra-high backswing like Pete Weber's in which your arm rises to a position virtually perpendicular to the floor.

To me, late timing is when the foot hits the floor on the next-to-

1997 PBA Hall of Fame inductee Dave Ferraro is late with his timing. *Photo by Dan Chidester, courtesy of the PBA*

last step but the ball is still rising during the backswing. Without an unnatural adjustment, the foot will beat the ball to the line. Only a bowler who possesses exceptional strength will be able to pull that ball through and get it to the line as the slide occurs. Obviously, it can be done because many bowlers who have very late timing have nevertheless done well. Harry Sullins was very late. Generally, players who plant instead of sliding are slightly late. Examples include 1992 PBA Player of the Year Dave Ferraro and Ron Palombi, Jr., who has claimed two-thirds of the Triple Crown by virtue of having won the 1990 U.S. Open and the 1993 PBA National Championship.

In contrast, veteran standout Ernie Schlegel is early with his timing. As Ernie takes the pivot (next to last) stride his ball is already descending. The danger with this technique is that being excessively early could cause the ball to slip from the player's hand, resulting in a shot with little power that could produce a pocket split.

I prefer to define timing in this way because this is how it was taught to me and it always made sense. In addition, it's a very simple way to measure if you are in time, late, or early. It's much harder to try to spot the foot-hand relationship at the foul line than it is at the earlier juncture of the delivery.

When I sense that my timing isn't right, I simply ask a fellow player to observe the position of my right foot as the ball has reached its zenith. Given that command, even a novice can usually spot any flaws.

Being out of Time

As far as I'm concerned, being in time is the way to go. Notwithstanding the handful of stars I cited earlier, being in time has historically been a common ingredient among almost all of the sport's top players. That is evidence of its significance. On almost every delivery, Walter Ray Williams is in time. So is the incomparable Earl Anthony. Ditto for Norm Duke, Don Johnson, Mike Aulby, and Marshall Holman. Add Dick Weber, plus his son, Pete, to the list.

And, yes, Mark Roth. Because of Mark's unorthodox style, which includes a high backswing and either six or seven steps (how many he took on a given day involved such random chance that I think it depended on the phase of the moon), many observers thought that his timing was late. In my role as a television commentator, I studied tapes of Mark in action. It didn't matter how many steps he took; his foot was almost always on the floor at the peak of his backswing.

I have never understood the logic of those who believe that late timing is preferable to proper timing. That school of thought claims that you can get more on the ball by being slightly late. The theory is that the planting foot provides a foundation as the player pulls the ball through the release point while snapping closed—rotating the upper body so the shoulders are parallel to the foul line as the ball is released.

Does being slightly late increase leverage? Perhaps, but only marginally so. However, the tradeoff is the need to employ a lot of muscle instead of letting gravity do the work. The more muscle one uses, the harder it is to be consistent. Another problem is the tendency to steer shots while under pressure.

Moreover, making such sacrifices for the sake of a little bit more power has never been less advisable than it is today. Bowling balls continue to improve exponentially. They have become so efficient at driving through the pins that the key to improving your average is to hit the pocket consistently. And there's no question whatsoever in my mind that proper timing is most conducive to achieving that objective.

MISTAKE 12

Believing It's Better Late than Never

What do bowling timing and showing up for a job interview have in common? In both cases, it's better to err on the side of arriving quite a bit early than to be even a little bit late.

Of course, it's always our intention to make a good shot with every delivery. Having said that, when you make a mistake you will discover that being slightly early is more forgiving than being slightly late. When you're early, with rare exception, your shot will still reach your target. When my timing got late, I had a tendency to hang in the thumb hole. The result was a poor roll and a shot that often went through the nose (ball hits center of headpin, usually leaving a split).

MISTAKE 13

Not Understanding the Components of Timing

Far too many players leave their timing to happenstance. The reason why it becomes such a problem when things go wrong is that not enough of us understand it sufficiently so as to make a technical adjustment when we're out of sync.

Use an imaginary table for your pushaway.

Correct timing starts with a proper execution of your pushaway. Remember the imaginary table that I spoke of on page 12. As you place your ball on that table, the foot on the same side as your bowling hand must hit the floor. This represents the first step for those of you who use a four-step delivery. For five-step players, this is your second step and it follows a very small stride with the opposite foot.

If you either drop the ball into your swing or hand it upward, you must make an adjustment in the timing of your stride. Although this can be done, it complicates your delivery. It's far easier to do it right and step while your ball is positioned in line with your target at waist height.

When the pushaway is executed correctly and gravity is allowed to rule your armswing, all that follows should be in time. Thus, the ball will be beside the same-side leg as your opposite foot hits the floor on your subsequent step. At most, the ball might be a few inches behind that leg during the backswing.

The conclusion of timing, by my definition, is during that next-to-last step (the third step for a four-step player or the fourth step for a five-step bowler). At this juncture the ball is at the peak of your backswing.

If you're in time, you have a far greater chance of executing a smooth release. Should you constantly miss your target, timing could quite possibly be the reason. Ask a teammate to keep an eye on your next delivery to ascertain whether that's the case.

Should you be out of time, consider these two corrections. One is to pay particular attention to your pushaway. If your timing has been consistently late, make certain to hand the ball forward—and not upward—so that it gets into the swing as the same-side foot hits the floor. When your timing is early,

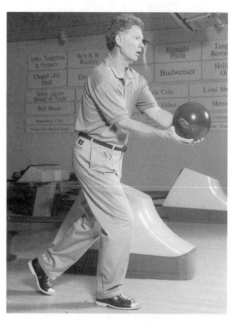

To correct late timing, start your pushaway prior to your initial stride.

make a conscious effort to hand the ball fully forward at waist height to prevent it from beginning the downswing too soon.

The other alternative is to adjust your footwork. For late timing, decrease the length of your first step. Remind yourself to move at a natural pace to the line as you may have been guilty of "running." If your timing is early, lengthen your first step.

Fix early timing by stepping first and putting the ball in motion second.

MISTAKE 14

Starting out of Sync

As noted, the right foot and the right hand (or left foot and left hand for you southpaws) move together. If your pushaway precedes that first step, your timing is immediately compromised. Unless your feet "run" to catch up with the ball, you will be early.

MISTAKE 15

Poor Conversions

It's always tricky to change the number of steps you take. This is especially the case when going from fewer steps to more. I've seen scores of three-step players suffer when making the transition to a four-step delivery. A prime cause of their misery is that they step with the foot without moving the ball. In essence, they're still performing a three-step delivery. However, quite often this step-first, pushaway-after sequence results in the ball being late.

MISTAKE 16

Swinging for the Fences

I love watching Pete Weber compete. But if I ever attempted to emulate his style, I'd probably be a candidate for shoulder surgery in short order.

A high backswing is fine if you have sufficient talent to remain in time. But not many players are able to pull off that trick. If your backswing is either excessive or, like Roy Buckley's, only waist high, I suggest the more conventional shoulder-high style. This will make it far easier for you to maintain consistent timing.

MISTAKE 17

Being a Race-ist

Many individual sports pit an athlete against a stopwatch, including track, auto racing, and swimming. Bowling, however, isn't among them.

But you'd never know that by watching some amateurs. Instead of allowing the ball to dictate their foot speed, they fly to the line like a sprinter charging out of the starting gate. Slow down! Let your feet move naturally. You'll find that doing so will help you improve your timing.

MISTAKE 18

Not Analyzing Every Shot

When all is said and done, bowling is a fairly simple game. But don't be lulled into assuming that it involves any less knowledge and thought than other sports. The fact is, essentially we all are our own coaches. Even at my level, in which top-class instructors are available to help us, no one knows my own game as well as I do. I am the only person who can feel what I'm doing wrong.

When you execute an errant shot, it is vital that you figure out the cause of the problem. Only when the flaw has been accurately identified can you make a correction to your subsequent deliveries.

To me, it's a crime when a bowler rolls three subpar games and subsequently says that his timing was off. In all of bowling, few aspects of the delivery are as easy to identify and as simple to correct. The sooner you accomplish that, the better you'll score.

Summary

After you finish reading this chapter, take a moment to glance at the common error chart in the appendix. You'll notice that in several circumstances late or early timing is listed as a possible problem. I find inconsistent timing to be especially prevalent among the middle- and lower-average bowlers who hit the lanes but once or twice in a typical week.

Even if you hardly ever practice, it shouldn't be a difficult challenge to maintain good timing. Now that you know how to recognize when you're late or early as well as how to compensate, it's my hope that from now on you'll be on time almost all of the time!

CHAPTER 3

The Armswing

To improve your armswing, you could study tapes of masterful players like Dick Weber, David Ozio, and Norm Duke and attempt to emulate them. Or you could skip the VCR route and take a page out of Sir Isaac Newton's book.

One of Newton's 17th-century theories asserted that all objects attract each other, with the total force depending on the size of the bodies and the distance separating them. When Newton outlined how masses of matter are attracted to each other, it's doubtful he was concerned with assisting bowlers to more effectively knock over pins. Little did he know that his theory would explain why minimizing the use of one's muscles is the key ingredient in a good armswing.

The armswing is the path that the ball travels prior to being released. Because it begins as the continuation of your pushaway, a proper pushaway is essential to producing a correct armswing. If you drew an imaginary line from the ball to the target at any point during the armswing, the line should be perfectly straight, intersecting the target. That's why you want your armswing to be straight.

To visualize the ideal, picture an apple attached to a string. Imagine holding the end of that string in one hand with the apple in the other. Pull the apple upward until the string is taut. As you release the apple, gravity will cause it to descend as it swings forward in a straight line.

Substitute your bowling arm for that string and your ball for the apple, with your shoulder serving as the fulcrum. That, in essence, is the principle

Rely on gravity, not your muscles, to achieve an ideal armswing.

by which the armswing works. If you permit gravity to have its way, the ball will come forward in a straight motion and in a predictable amount of time.

To hear professional bowlers discussing their armswings, one would almost expect them to invoke quotations from Abraham Lincoln. The word that's used over and over is *free*. The freedom that they all seek is from control of the swing by their arm muscles. The freer your armswing becomes, the more likely you'll be able to perform at your best when the pressure is mounting. Gravity will never choke!

Does this mean that a bowler with a "muscled" armswing can't be successful? Certainly not. Remember, the key to bowling is the consistent repetition of a series of motions. Doing something that is considered by conventional wisdom to be wrong can work as long as that "mistake" is repeated shot after shot. In fact, several pro stars who rely more on power than on accuracy for their success do employ a lot of muscle in their swings.

However—and this is key—they have to possess the psychological strength to remain composed on key shots. If they become tense, their muscles will tighten. When that happens, they are far more likely to veer the armswing off line and out of sync. Quite often that will result in pulling the shot inside of the target.

That's a key reason why, in my opinion, the ideal technique involves your arm muscles moving the ball only at the very beginning (the pushaway) and just before the conclusion (the release) of your swing. All that transpires between those two junctures should be fully dictated by the laws of gravity.

By allowing gravity to have its way, the game becomes easier, simpler, and more predictable. Conversely, combatting the principles of gravity distorts movements. This makes a straight arm movement far more difficult to achieve. It also can cause one to squeeze the ball, hindering a good release.

When gravity moves the ball throughout the swing, it also aids a natural tendency for our bodies to maintain a rhythm between our arms and legs. This helps to make our timing more consistent.

Taller players with long wingspans, such as Dave Davis, usually move their feet more slowly. This is because the arm travels a longer path, which in turn requires more time between the pushaway and the release. Conversely, bowlers with short arms tend to move their feet more rapidly (with some variance based on the height of one's backswing).

Being tall, like former PBA star Steve Cook, requires adjusting one's footwork to remain in time. *Courtesy of the PBA*

No matter what, the key is to let gravity—and *not* your muscles—do the work. This will create an effortlessness that will help you achieve peak performance over several games without fatigue. Aside from feeling less tired at the end of an evening of play, you will have less stress on your arm and shoulder which, in turn, should promote injury-free play and aid your longevity. Quite simply, this is the easiest, simplest, and most reliable way to play this game.

It's no accident that Dick Weber, the only man to have captured at least one PBA title in five different decades, is often referred to by his peers as "the man with the golden armswing." Earl Anthony may not feature classic technique, given that his left elbow is bent, but he doesn't use a lot of muscle and his motions appear effortless. As I write this, Earl is approaching his 60th birthday and he's still a force whenever he competes, even against players half his age. Dave Davis, who won Senior Masters titles back-to-back, has a classic free swing. So does Hall of Fame member David Ozio.

Although I believe this to be the key factor in allowing most players to realize their potential, let me reiterate that no "rules" of how to bowl are cast in stone. Walter Ray

A superior armswing was one of the many outstanding attributes of all-time superstar Dick Weber. *Courtesy of the PBA*

Williams is as good a player as has ever laced up a pair of bowling shoes, and his armswing is no more free than are box seats to a Cleveland Indians game.

Walter, however, is a unique individual. He's a fabulous talent who is a dominant star in two sports (having captured several world horseshoes-pitching championships). Aside from uncanny accuracy, Walter's mixture of muscle usage with gravity works for him because he's a remarkably disciplined and confident athlete. I've joined him on the links and I can report that although he's no threat to Tiger Woods, he still approaches golf the same way he does horseshoes and bowling. He is as confident a human being as I have ever encountered. Everything he does is aggressive. There isn't one ounce of tentativeness in his game. While he has some finesse, that certainly will never be considered his hallmark.

Watching Walter bowl, you will notice that his arm accelerates at the bottom of his swing just prior to his release. He comes through the ball the way General William Tecumseh Sherman went through the Georgian countryside. And, as with General Sherman, very little is left standing when Walter comes through town.

However, Walter's swing is certainly not muscled to the degree that many amateurs use their muscles to guide the ball. But it is far more muscled than, say, Norm Duke's.

Although Norm and Walter Ray are demonstrably different in this regard, there are no absolutes. No player's swing is 100 percent muscled, as it's impossible to violate Newton's law. And no player's armswing is fully free. However, striving to obtain maximum freedom remains a goal that, while not fully obtainable, will greatly improve your game. It all must begin with a good pushaway. As stated in Chapter 1, you should visualize a table in front of your bowling arm. Your job is to place your ball on that table.

The removal of the supporting hand allows gravity to go to work for you.

Remember, your pushaway coincides with stepping with the same-side foot. Thus, the right-handed player strides with the right foot as soon as the ball is fully extended forward. At the same time, your nonbowling hand, which had supported the ball, is removed from it. At precisely this point, gravity goes to work as the ball drops into a natural swing.

If you hold the ball by your side in correct position during the pushaway, it can travel in a straight line without hitting the side of your body. This will make it possible for the entire arch to align with your target.

You must be aware of several factors that comprise a strong armswing, as well as pitfalls that you must avoid.

MISTAKE 19

Poor Address Position

For bowling purposes, Mr. Shakespeare had it backward. In our sport, all is well that *starts* well.

As noted, holding the ball in front of your stomach or chest during the address virtually guarantees a poor armswing. In order for the ball to clear your hips during the backswing, it will have to be handed out away from your body. If this is the case, your arm won't move in a straight line.

Make certain that the ball is lined up with your shoulder, with your non-bowling hand helping to support the weight. The height at which the ball is held will affect the length of your armswing—assuming that you allow gravity to do its part, the higher the ball is held, the faster it will fall and the farther back it will come. This is why changing the height at which the ball is held is a common adjustment that advanced players use to alter their shot's speed.

A solid pushaway.

Pathetic Pushaway

If the objective of a pushaway is to place the ball on an imaginary table, the pushaway featured by the great majority of players would shatter every glass on the table. Far too many players shove the ball forward. It's hard enough to disengage one's muscles after executing a proper pushaway. It's virtually impossible to do so when the pushaway is poor and isn't smooth.

Some players hand the ball upward. This isn't an inherently fatal flaw, although a high pushaway would represent a handicap to most players.

So, too, dropping the ball downward instead of laying it on that imaginary table will negatively affect your armswing, placing the ball into the swing too soon. As a result, your feet will have to move more rapidly to catch up. Or you'll have to use muscle to slow down your armswing to get back in time. Neither option is conducive to consistency.

This high pushaway may be fine for Mike Aulby, but it doesn't do anything for my game!

Dropping the ball instead of handing it out will compromise your timing and, quite likely, cost you leverage at the foul line.

If your pushaway is right, the ball should be at the side of your same-side leg as your second stride hits the approach. In the case of a right-handed player, this occurs as the left foot hits the floor. The hand and bowling arm should be as relaxed as possible.

MISTAKE 21

High Backswing

During my next-to-last step the ball reaches the peak of my backswing. My recommendation is that the ball approach only shoulder height.

Once again, there are exceptions to this rule. Pete Weber and Amleto Monacelli are contemporary examples of top-flight players with high backswings. In my day, 6'7" Steve Cook's backswing was a threat to low-flying aircraft.

However, not many of us can be like them. The higher the ball moves, the more likely it will veer off line. And this doesn't even take into consideration the wear and tear that a high backswing can inflict on one's shoulder.

If you are to err on the altitude of the ball, it's better to be short rather than high. Hall of Famers Roy Buckley and Billy Hardwick both fell in this category. Although they couldn't match many others for striking power, they were extremely accurate. As such, they rarely beat themselves.

Here's a tip that may sound odd, but that I guarantee will help to restrict the height of your armswing. Lock your chin in a level position and jut that chin forward as if you

Like the majority of players, my backswing reaches shoulder height.

To keep your armswing from escaping, lock your chin.

were to walk up to someone and say, "Go ahead, hit me, I dare you!" This will help keep your armswing in check.

What Goes up Must Come Down

The zenith of the backswing represents another problematic point for many players. The natural tendency is to reach back for the proverbial "something extra" at this juncture of the delivery. We tend to visualize a strike with pins flying everywhere. Like a golfer trying to get an extra 15 yards on a drive, the desire to prematurely add force to the swing often leads to disastrous results. If your delivery has been correct up to this point, there is no reason to do anything unnatural by adding extra force. Take a cue from the Beatles and remind yourself to just "Let It Be."

Remember, that bowling ball isn't exactly a light object. If you doubt that gravity can propel it downward at a sufficient pace, then try this experiment. Put your fingers and thumb in the ball holes. While standing still, lift the ball behind you to the approximate spot of the top of your backswing. Now, hold the ball in that position.

I can guarantee you that the ball won't stay there for long. I doubt if you'll be able to maintain that position for more than a split second. Trust me—gravity will bring your ball down in a straight line toward the target.

Not Stepping on the Pedal

Just because muscle shouldn't be introduced at the top of the backswing doesn't mean that gravity must do *all* of the work. As the ball moves forward

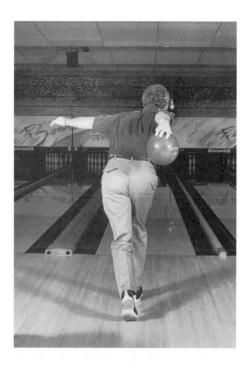

A straight armswing ensures a shot that's on target.

and drops below shoulder height, think about completing the swing. At this point the ball is already moving toward the target. Accelerate through the ball, imagining your hand chasing that ball.

This is why not introducing muscle until the right time is so helpful. If you don't have freedom throughout most of the swing, sometimes the ball will decelerate at the point of release. That will hinder your thumb from making a clean and timely exit from the ball. Without a proper release, you are virtually guaranteed that the resulting shot will be dead when it arrives at the pins.

MISTAKE 24

Not Following Through to the Target

As the ball leaves your hand, your arm continues on its path toward your target. Your follow-through is directed toward your aiming point. My focus is to follow through at my target and upward toward the ceiling.

The follow-through should be the same in every situation.

Some players bend the elbow after the release. This may not win you any style points, but bowling, unlike gymnastics, isn't about looking pretty. Doing what comes naturally to you is fine as long as you do it consistently and it doesn't hamper your performance. My elbow "breaks" and my bowling hand tends to fly past my right ear. Walter Ray Williams's follow-through makes him look like a tree in late autumn whose barren branches point in every direction. I suspect that this decided lack of post-shot elegance hasn't caused an appreciable loss of sleep to a four-time PBA Player of the Year whose average official annual income topped $149,000 from

1986–96 (a figure, incidentally, that as of 1997 was higher than all but six of the 33 other performance category members of the PBA Hall of Fame claimed during their most productive years).

Yes, folks, it's true that bowling is not about "how"—it's about "how many."

Summary

The more conventional your style, the easier it will be for you to repeat the motion. The more you can duplicate movements, the better your average should be.

If there's one area in which many lower-average players fall short, it is in having too much muscle in the armswing. Let's use a scale of 1 to 10, with 1 representing all muscle and 10 being full freedom of movement. The ideal armswing would fall in the 7 to 8 range. It would be a 10 from the conclusion of the pushaway until the ball's descent from the top of the backswing. It would probably be a 4 during the pushaway, and about a 5 during the release and follow-through stages.

Using excessive muscle can lead to the swing being off line. It also forces you to work to match the speed of your footwork to that of the armswing. It leads many to a death grip on the ball, making the forearm as tight as Jack Benny's purse strings and the swing as controlled as a voter in the old Soviet Union.

CHAPTER 4

The Release

Many attributes separate higher-average bowlers from those with lower averages. Having observed countless individuals in both categories, I have come to appreciate the importance of a strong release. The Bible states that love covers a multitude of sins. Likewise, a good hand release covers a multitude of mistakes.

Without exception, every top professional player releases the ball in a consistent and productive manner. There are several different varieties of releases: semi-roller, full-roller, spinner, and back-up ball. Their common ingredient is that better players get this vital aspect of the game right on virtually every shot.

Semi-Roller

The semi-roller, also known as the three-quarter–roller, is by a wide margin the most popular release of today's higher-average players. It's the choice of almost every pro star. One of its many selling points is that it can be used on a wide variety of lane conditions. Versatility is achieved merely by increasing or

The ideal thumb-first, fingers-later release.

The semi-roller's track.

decreasing the amount of pre-release hand rotation or by throwing the shot faster or slower.

The semi-roller produces shots that grip the lane effectively. As such, a well-executed delivery will produce a shot that drives through the pins with minimal deflection. This results in a great carry percentage for both solid pocket shots and for half-hits.

The semi-roller tracks to the left of both the thumb and the finger holes (in other words, if you held the ball's face upward, as shown in the photo, the ring represents the surface of the ball that comes in contact with the lane). The track is to the right of the thumb and finger holes for a left-handed player.

To produce this release, a right-handed bowler's thumb should rotate in a counterclockwise direction. It is positioned at approximately 2 o'clock throughout the armswing. At the bottom of the swing, as the thumb exits, it rotates to about the 11 o'clock position. The clockwise rotation of a left-handed bowler's thumb is from 10 o'clock to 1 o'clock.

The timing of the hand rotation is important. A premature turn will prevent your thumb from a clean exit and will guarantee a weak release. I constantly remind myself to wait as long as I can.

Full-Roller

The full-roller tracks between the thumb and the finger holes, as shown in the photo, were especially popular in the era of rubber balls and lacquer lanes. At that time it was common to face a "track condition" in which a succession of shots around the second arrow quite literally wore a path to the pocket. Placing the ball in that zone allowed the lane to help steer the ball right into the pocket.

During the 1970s, several PBA events were won by players using a full-roller who aimed between the second and the third arrows. Although the full-roller is nearly extinct on the pro circuits, it remains an option on certain lane conditions. This is especially the case if you can see that a track shot exists.

On the PBA and LPBT (Ladies Pro Bowlers Tour) levels, however, it's rarely used. Having said that, as I write this it's only been a few months since Don Helling won a senior event by employing a full-roller.

This grip involves imagining shaking someone's hand. The thumb begins at about 10 o'clock and exits after moving clockwise toward 12 o'clock. (A southpaw rotates coun-

The full-roller's track.

terclockwise from 2 o'clock to 12 o'clock). When coaching right-handed bowlers on this technique, I advise them to envision turning a doorknob to the right.

When my career was getting started in the late 1960s, the dominant player was Billy Hardwick. A two-time PBA Player of the Year (1963 and 1969), he used a full-roller to capture 17 titles. He also won professional bowling's Triple Crown—the 1963 PBA National Championship, the 1965 Tournament of Champions, and the 1969 Bowling Proprietors Association of America (BPAA) All-Star (the forerunner to today's U.S. Open).

Naturally, during my rookie season on the Tour in 1967, I emulated the release that was being used by Hardwick and most of the top stars of that time. That year I won the Tampa Sertoma Open and the Youngstown Open. (Editor's note: While becoming the PBA's top rookie, Mike finished among that year's top 10 money winners. As of this book's publication date, no freshman since has duplicated that feat.) By the end of the 1968 Summer Tour, I had added a third title by winning in El Paso. By any measure, that start more than exceeded my expectations.

The full-roller (not to mention greasy hair!) was in vogue when this rookie hit the PBA Tour. *Courtesy of the PBA*

Even with my success, I realized that the full-roller would soon go the way of the dinosaur. I could sense that its carrying power was limited. No matter how much I practiced or tinkered with its nuances, I simply couldn't make it hit hard enough at the back end to carry half-hits. Moreover, it wasn't a sufficiently flexible release. I would leave more soft 10 pins than I cared to remember when I had to play an inside line in which my target was to the left of the 12th board.

When I mentioned my sentiments to several peers, they looked at me as if I were the Tour's leading candidate for psychiatric help. Bowlers tend to be conservative, and risk-taking is usually seen as the last resort of the desperate player. In my case, conventional wisdom insisted, if it ain't broke, don't fix it.

Nevertheless, I was convinced that I would have to drastically revamp my release if I were to remain competitive on a long-term basis. I approached respected coach Bill Taylor to enlist his help.

After having made the change to a semi-roller, it took a full year of constant practice to become fully comfortable with it. Not until the midway point of the 1970 Tour would I win again. I slipped to 27th in official winnings for 1969. While I needed the money, I viewed my short-term sacrifice as an investment in Mike and Debbie Durbin's future.

Meanwhile, I wasn't exactly receiving yeoman support from my peers. Scores of pros told me that I was making a huge miscalculation. The only backing I got was from Debbie, and that was based solely on her feeling that she should remain loyal to and be supportive of her husband. Anyone with any degree of bowling expertise was convinced that my rack was short a few pins.

I'm glad that I had the courage not to be swayed. I have since realized that pro bowlers tend to discount any unorthodox technique. When Earl

Anthony made his Tour debut, the conventional wisdom was that his bent elbow would prevent him from going far. So, too, with Mark Roth's seven-step, high-backswing style. The 75 titles between them on the National Tour (no other individual is even approaching the 30-win plateau) prove that sometimes it pays to follow one's instincts.

Time has proven my thesis on the release to have been correct. Yes, the full-roller can still work when the lane conditions are suitable. As such, it must be considered an added weapon that the versatile high-average player should have in her arsenal. Unless a player is able to practice often, it's tough to even master one type of release. If you are picking one entrée from the menu of bowling releases, I strongly recommend going the semi-roller route. There's no question in my mind that it's the way to go for the foreseeable future.

Spinner

Option number three (both in order of prominence and efficiency) is the spinner. It causes the ball to gyrate down the lane like a top. Note the very small track ring that it features (see photo). As such, it generates precious little inertia and tends to deflect after contacting the pins. Although today's superior equipment does negate some of those considerations, it still greatly handicaps carry percentage.

The one situation in which it can be effective is when the lanes are extremely dry. This occurs after many games have been rolled without dressing being applied to the lane. On occasion, a night block of a PBA or LPBT event sees shots hooking too much.

On such a condition, the spinner release will cause your ball to travel far down the lane before it begins to

The spinner's track is the smallest of the three prominent options, so your ball won't grip the lane as efficiently.

grip the surface. In an earlier era, it was widely used when competing on a shellac finish, a very porous lane surface. The great Hank Marino, who was honored as bowling's top performer of the first half of the 20th century, threw a spinner.

If you're a right-handed bowler, rotate your thumb counterclockwise from 2 o'clock to 9 o'clock. A left-handed bowler does the opposite, rotating clockwise from 10 o'clock to 3 o'clock.

Back-Up Ball

The fourth option is the back-up ball. It's also often referred to as a *reverse hook*. However, that expression is somewhat deceptive because the back-up cannot generate nearly as powerful a roll as the real McCoy. With one's hand behind the ball, the fingers and thumb move clockwise as the thumb goes under the ball (counterclockwise for a lefty).

I consider it to be a major flaw for a player to throw a back-up ball as his or her shot of choice. But it, too, has its place. A handful of women pros use it to get a better angle on shooting a 10-pin spare. PBA Hall of Fame member and 1980 Player of the Year Wayne Webb has used it to con-

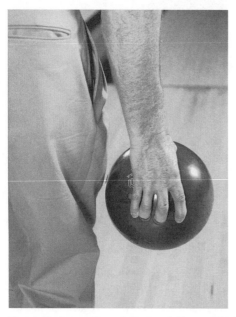 

The clockwise motion of the hand (for a right-handed player) results in a back-up ball.

vert the 2-8-10 split. I've seen Wayne fooling around with it in practice, and he's pretty good at it.

MISTAKE 25

A Thumb That Overstays Its Welcome

The key principle of a good release is that your thumb must exit the ball prior to the fingers. This holds true for all varieties of releases, and it represents the most common shortcoming among amateur bowlers. Either the thumb and the fingers leave simultaneously, or the differential is so minimal as to be inconsequential.

The sequential exit (thumb first, fingers later) is essential. Without it, you roll a dead ball that has very little hook and even less carrying power. But don't take my word for it; the pins that you leave will tell you.

In contrast, a higher-average player's release allows for maximum "lift." As the photograph clearly illustrates, the thumb should leave the ball at the bottom of the armswing. With your eyes riveted on the target, shoulders square to the foul line, and body well balanced, the ball still hangs on the fingers. That hang allows you to impart a "heavy" roll on the strike shot to improve carrying power. A heavy roll that's imparted by a good hand release sees the ball roll through the pins with little or no deflection.

A simple thought pattern can help you execute this properly. As you are about to let the ball go, think of letting go with your thumb but not with your fingers. Hey, I said it was simple!

In order for this to occur, your thumb cannot be pointed at the

A good release involves several factors.

Thumbs down to any release in which your thumb is pointed downward.

floor. Because it must be behind the ball, your fingers will be beneath the ball.

As a teenager I received a great piece of advice. I was about 15 and I used a full-roller. Part of my daily routine was to practice at Airway Alleys, an eight-lane center in Burbank, California, that was owned by my parents. Since I was already carrying a 200 average, I benefited from the advice of many veterans who viewed me as a player with some potential.

One of the scratch bowlers from Airway's Classic League told me to apply pressure with my middle two fingers, but not to let go with those fingers. Be certain to maintain that pressure during the bottom of my swing, he said, and to force the bowling ball to open up my fingers. Doing so would impart lift and allow my shots to have a "heavy" roll.

MISTAKE 26

Acting Naturally

What could possibly be wrong with a release that feels natural? After all, didn't I say that you should be relaxed throughout your delivery?

To a degree, this is important. But comfort shouldn't be achieved at the expense of competence. The back-up ball just isn't a viable option. Even so, many beginning female players throw it.

For years I couldn't understand why the back-up is fairly prevalent among neophyte women but virtually nonexistent among male bowlers. Then I noticed that the difference is in how most men and women naturally position their arms while at rest. A man's hands are usually adjacent to his legs with the palms facing inward, while many women hold their arms away

Here's a close-up of the hand motion that's used to throw the popular semi-roller.

from their legs with their hands pointed outward. When a woman puts her hand behind a ball, the natural tendency is to rotate the thumb away from the body. Thus, the back-up ball.

If that's you, it will be very difficult to train yourself to move your thumb in a counterclockwise motion (or clockwise, if you are left-handed). Even so, I have taught scores of women to throw a hook by teaching them the full-roller. For whatever reason, they are able to learn it with far greater ease than a semi-roller.

To ease the transition, I just remind them to hold the ball as if it's a suitcase with the thumb at 10 o'clock (2 o'clock for a lefty). I tell them to swing it in that position throughout the entire delivery. Releasing the ball with the hand so aligned will produce a full-roller that features a gentle hook.

MISTAKE 27

Lack of Leverage

I struggle to think of any sport in which a ball may be propelled efficiently without having proper balance and leverage. So, too, in bowling. The relationship of the ball to your body at the bottom of the armswing is a vital ingredient. The greater the distance between the ankle of your sliding foot and the ball, the less leverage. Less leverage means a ball that rolls weakly.

If gravity is controlling your armswing, the ball will swing straight and will be near your ankle as the thumb exits (see photo). The ball will be far removed from the ankle only if excessive muscle has been used.

As you enter into your slide, the ball should be directly beneath your bowling shoulder. It's at that point that the thumb leaves the ball. Your fingers will remain inside their respective holes until the start of the upswing.

I think it's only fair to report that not every expert concurs with my sentiments. John Jowdy, who is one of the premier coaches of the game, teaches his students not to hit the release on the upswing. It's his theory that the ball should land on a lane the way an airplane lands on a runway. He claims that is a key consideration to consistent scoring on today's lane conditions.

Whether you go the Jowdy route or the Durbin route, having leverage and being balanced at the bottom of the swing are vital.

The proximity of the ball to the inside of the ankle of the sliding foot increases leverage and, with it, carrying power.

MISTAKE 28

Squeezing the Fruit While Being Watched

Treat that bowling ball as if it were a tomato in your supermarket while the produce manager peeks over your shoulder. As the old toilet paper commercials implored, please don't squeeze the product.

Under pressure, we all tend to squeeze the ball or turn it early. Either way, you won't exit from the ball cleanly. Here's a solution—concentrate on leading with your ring finger toward your target. That will force you to stay behind the ball longer.

MISTAKE 29

Throwing Three-Quarter 100 Percent the Same

The several different ways to produce a semi-roller all make the ball react differently. The best method is to visualize your hand behind the ball with your fingers at 6 o'clock. As you release, think of those fingers making a one-quarter counterclockwise turn from 6 to 3 o'clock (lefties turn clockwise from

The slight rotation needed for the three-quarter roller.

6 to 9 o'clock). This will give you as much power as the average bowler will ever need. It's done primarily with a firm and straight wrist so that your shot makes a gentle arc to the pocket. In general, it's better if you don't cover a tremendous number of boards (because doing so makes being consistently accurate more difficult) or go dead straight (which can hinder your carrying power). As a general rule, the shot should make its move toward the pocket at the back end of the lane.

The tucked finger.

Another option is to place the fingers at 6 o'clock with the little finger tucked against the ball. Insert the fingers into the ball, but they should barely rotate, remaining in the 6 o'clock position or, at most, moving to 5 o'clock (7 o'clock for lefties).

When the back ends are dry, try the straight release.

This is a very straight release that produces a forward end-over-end roll with a slight hook. It's very effective when you are faced with dry back ends. It will enable you to be accurate while still assuring that your shot will hit with ample power (especially when you're able to play to the right of the 13th board).

I used this release to win a lot of PBA events and it's the same one I use for spares because it helps me throw the ball straight. Another selling point is that it's relatively easy to repeat time after time, which appeals to my conservative nature. For those of you who golf, I see it as the equivalent of hitting a 3-wood down the middle of the fairway as opposed to spraying my driver. That's why I often refer to it as my "3-wood release."

I also often use it when playing a far outside line in which it's necessary to go up the boards. If I really need to decrease or delay the hook, I will not place my fingers quite as far into the holes. I also untuck that little finger and bring the index finger in closer.

For a more powerful option, cup your wrist. Your hand is behind the ball with your fingers still at 6 o'clock. Just before your thumb exits, your hand rolls upward. As your fingers let go of the ball (with your wrist remaining cupped throughout the entire swing), imagine your hand chasing

The angle of your wrist—flat (left), broken, or cupped (right)—will change how much your shot will hook.

the ball. That will force you to keep the wrist cupped, which produces a heavy roll and a bigger hook at the back end. Believe it or not, the difference can be as much as a five- or six-board adjustment in where you must stand on the approach.

Your nonbowling fingers (the ones not inserted into the ball) can be positioned so as to have your shot finish harder on the back end, which upgrades your power. Place the middle and ring fingers snugly into the holes up to their first joints. Next, tuck your little finger under the ball. This will make your ring finger move inward, which will automatically give you lift. Spread the index finger away from the finger holes. This will keep the ball in the palm of the hand and enable you to get around the side of the ball more as you're letting it go.

In fact, several power players actually lift with their index fingers. This makes the shot go farther down the lane and finish harder with a heavier roll. Those are important considerations when playing an inside line.

Some stars, like the great Mark Roth, develop a callous on the base of their index fingers! That's because Mark produced a violent snapping motion with his entire hand after his thumb had exited from his ball. In contrast, the skin on my index finger has always been as soft as a baby's skin! Again, to borrow a golf term, think of this as your "driver" release.

If you can develop these three releases and execute them well even while under pressure, there will be almost no condition in which you can't score. The most versatile players on the PBA Tour in the 1990s have been Norm Duke and Walter Ray Williams, who both excel while utilizing several varieties of releases mastering speed control.

For decades I believed that the all-time greatest bowler when it came to changing releases was the

Ron Palombi, Jr.'s powerful release has made him a star. *Courtesy of the* PBA

late Billy Welu. It's only a slight exaggeration to suggest that he could do anything with a bowling ball. A close second to Billy was ABC Hall of Fame member Sarge Easter. Don Johnson was very good during his prime.

As good as that trio was, I don't think I've seen anybody more versatile and flexible at releases than Walter Ray Williams and Norm Duke. Mr. Williams is simply amazing; he can beat other players on their preferred condition by hooking the ball or throwing it straight, by throwing it fast or slow, and by playing the gutter or a deep inside line.

Be aware that you can partially compensate for a lack of physical versatility through equipment changes. Details on doing that via wrist devices can be found starting on page 89.

MISTAKE 30

Always Taking Moses's Advice

Biblical admonishments notwithstanding, thou shalt kill; at least, kill your hook on spare attempts in which accuracy is vital but power isn't a factor.

The less you hook your shot, the less susceptible it is to the whims of unpredictable oil migration. Oil moves during play. Because it's invisible you can't see which parts of the lane have become dry (where the ball will over-react) or oily (and not allow a hook). By rolling the ball end-over-end, it will go straight in either situation. I would hate to discover after missing a cross-lane 10 pin spare attempt that the left side of the lane was either drier or oilier than I had thought. A ball that rolls end-over-end and goes straight is far more likely to reach its intended destination.

Think of it this way—Bowler A normally covers two boards on a single-pin spare, but Bowler B crosses six. If a different segment of the lane is so dry as to double the amount of hook, Bowler A will now cover four boards (with the shot two inches off the center of the pin) while Bowler B will hook over twelve boards (and will be six inches wide of target). You have a five-board margin of error, so A gets an "A" for making the spare while B must overcome an open frame.

To kill a shot, veteran pro Gary Dickinson removes his ring finger from the ball and lays it over its normal hole. Or don't insert your fingers in as deep as usual, so that the pads of the fingertips rest in the edge of the holes.

This forces you to hold the two other fingers closer together. I use a 6 o'clock release with absolutely no rotation. Yet another option is to drop your thumb so that it points to the floor at the point of release. Marshall Holman uses the spinner release. My recommendation is to employ some old-fashioned trial and error until you discover what works best for you.

Summary

Having a wide variety of releases is a prerequisite for success. While most league players throw the ball only one way, your ability to hone different methods will enable you to improve your game. At the very least, you should have a preferred release for your strike ball, and a kill shot for covering non–double-wood spares.

My recommendation on strike shots is to use the semi-roller. If possible, you should strive to become comfortable doing that while altering your wrist position (bent back, flat, or cupped). Regardless of which option you pick for a particular shot, a sequential ball exit (thumb first, fingers next) and adequate leverage are necessary to produce a powerful roll.

CHAPTER 5

The Finish

Watch a dozen bowlers in action and you'll see a dozen different ways to get to the foul line. Even on the LPBT and PBA Tours you'll see a wide variety of styles.

The athletic parallel that comes to mind is hitting a baseball. I once read an article by the great Ted Williams in which he analyzed various batting styles. Although many of them seemed to be dissimilar, Williams noted that several key common ingredients were featured by the game's best hitters during the most important parts of the swing.

So, too, in bowling. The best players have a straight armswing and are square to the foul line during the point of release. They hold the head steady throughout the delivery with their eyes riveted on the target. Their movements are rhythmic and they are well balanced at the foul line.

No matter how different players may look as they approach the foul line, the better bowlers tend to have a lot in common as they finish the shot. Those ingredients include bending the nonsliding knee, bringing the sliding foot under the chin, pointing the opposite arm toward the opposite wall, a hand release in which the thumb flies out of the ball prior to the imparting of force and lift by the fingers, eyes locked on the target, and the arm following through to the ceiling.

A solid finish is an essential factor in bowling well on a consistent basis. It begins with the next-to-last step and doesn't end until after your ball has crossed the arrows.

MISTAKE 31

Failing to Be Well Balanced

In order to impart any appreciable amount of impetus to your strike shot, you must produce leverage at the point of release. This is only possible if you are well balanced as the ball leaves your hand.

An important part of that process is to produce a counterweight to that rather heavy object that you're about to roll. As my downswing commences, my nonbowling arm is raised and is pointed at the opposite wall. Maintaining that posture until well after the ball is released helps to maintain balance. Conversely, the failure to do so makes it very difficult to be solid at the point of the delivery when it matters the most.

MISTAKE 32

Staying Upright Too Long

A popular coaching tip is to "walk tall" to the foul line. That's good advice during the backswing, but it's not the right technique when the downswing is in progress.

At that point, it's time to get low. My conscious thought is to gradually bend my right knee as I take that next-to-last stride (lefties bend their left knee). Doing so will create a slight imbalance in my body. My body senses that, so the nonbowling foot comes to my rescue. The sliding foot will naturally be redirected slightly inward toward the center of my body. For ideal balance, it should be directly under the chin as the shot is being released.

Okay, so I've forgotten to bring along my ball, but the point is that one should walk tall to the line.

This technique is known as "filling the hole" that exists between the legs. You do so by pushing the slide underneath your chin. This is crucial as it will get you on balance to set you up for proper leverage. It also helps the downswing.

Try this experiment to prove my point. Stand tall and place your right hand behind you at shoulder height. Now, bend your right knee. What happened? Your right arm automatically came down to about hip high. The same principle applies to filling the hole. As that slide begins, with your weight on the balls of the sliding foot, your arm will effortlessly come forward on line.

Bend that knee to begin a gradual descent.

Thus, the bending of the knee helps with the downswing. By creating that moderate imbalance to force the opposite foot to fill the hole, you end up with

Filling the hole.

Even taller than Del Warren is Steve Cook. Both pros had to make a concerted effort to descend gradually and smoothly. *Courtesy of the* PBA

better balance. This puts you on line with the target, which helps with the follow-through.

Another result of bending the nonsliding knee is that as your body slowly descends, the knee of the sliding leg will automatically bend. That's especially true for shorter people. This action enables you to obtain better leverage at the line.

This important motion doesn't come nearly as easily to players who are tall. Veteran PBA star Del Warren has often struggled with this aspect of his game. Del is long (6′4″) and lean (185 pounds). In order to get low at the line, he experimented with several solutions before discovering that by positioning his head and his shoulders in front of his bending knee he would be able to go into the shot instead of pulling out of it.

If you're looking for a role model, try David Ozio. His descent and slide are as smooth as silk. This allows him to be consistently clean with his release as any player in the game today.

MISTAKE 33

Only Donuts and Bagels Should Have Holes

What would happen if you don't fill the hole? When the slide goes to the left of your body's center you will fall off balance to the right and the ball, generally, will go left of the target (vice versa for southpaws).

Very infrequently players "overfill" the hole. In that case the slide comes in past the center of the body toward the bowling shoulder (right shoulder for right-handers; left for left-handers). The result is cracking the ankle with the bowling ball. Trust me, you'll correct that quickly!

MISTAKE 34

Poor Sliding Technique

Ideally, you want the toes of your sliding foot to be perpendicular to the foul line. This is a detail that is ignored by most amateurs. When your toes point inward, your opposite hip (the left hip for a right-handed player) will rotate in the direction of your bowling hand. The shoulder of your bowling hand will then move backward, which will throw your armswing off line.

If you must make a mistake, it's better if the heel of the sliding foot moves inward (toward the shoulder of the bowling arm). In bowling parlance, this is known as *posting the shot*. I've been known to do that, as has PBA Hall of Fame member Nelson Burton, Jr. This helps to keep the body perfectly square to the line during the release. The only negative is that if the heel is to hit the floor with too great an impact, it will stop one from sliding.

If you must make a mistake with the angle of your sliding foot, posting represents the lesser of two evils.

Posting can be used intentionally to correct a situation in which your non-bowling shoulder is going too far forward so as to cause you to be virtually sideways to the line.

MISTAKE 35

Failing to Hold the Pose

A mental image that I try to paint for my students is posing for a picture after the ball has been released. Contrary to some people's opinions, your follow-through does matter.

Your objective is to achieve a 90-degree angle between your shoulder and forearm as it comes up on the follow-through, with your elbow bent and your palm facing your body or the opposite wall. Anything inside of 90 degrees (that is, closer to your body) causes the ball to hit with less power; anything outside of 90 degrees (that is, farther from your body) will generally cause the ball to hook high. These basic principles are why it's possible to predict the outcome of a shot by watching a bowler's post-shot pose.

In my opinion, the follow-through is the least studied aspect of the game, even at the professional level. Most of us simply do not watch the follow-through, and we especially don't watch it when shooting a spare. Ironically, most spare follow-throughs are perfect because there's no pressure.

Holding the pose is a good reminder when you wish to concentrate on executing a good follow-through.

A classic example of how a follow-through provided a barometer of how a player was faring was Carmen Salvino. When he was throwing the ball well, Carmen was relaxed and confident. The result was a perfect 90-degree angle during his follow-through. But on certain occasions, his arm would look more like a chicken wing as it deviated to the inside. When that happened, his ball wouldn't hit hard or it wouldn't get to the headpin.

When I'm serving as a television analyst, I always pay close attention to how that bowler follows through during warm-ups, when there is absolutely no pressure to perform. If his follow-through differs in the game, I know what's going on in his mind and how fast his heart is racing.

The greatest pressure bowler I ever saw was Dick Ritger. His follow-through was the same in a practice session as it was when he needed a strike to claim one of the 20 PBA titles he won.

I can still recall a test that was performed in Milwaukee during the 1970s in which medical professionals monitored the heart rates of both Ritger and Nelson Burton, Jr., during competition. Against all odds, Burton shot a perfect game while being hooked up. By the 12th shot, his pulse was astronomical. Like virtually all of us, he was excited and, I'm sure, a bit nervous.

As well as Burton bowled, Ritger rolled better. Dick produced 18 consecutive strikes. Far more amazing is that his heart rate never deviated one iota until he finally missed. He

Like a tell-all book, Carmen Salvino's follow-through was very revealing. *Courtesy of the PBA*

had an amazing ability to be "Mr. Ice" in pressure situations.

Just what does being cool in the clutch have to do with a good follow-through? Only everything! Having that ball on line at the top of the swing is important but it isn't a guarantee that you'll make a quality shot. The player who is nervous will try to put something extra on the ball or will attempt to steer it to the pocket.

The next time you bowl in your league, make it a point to observe the follow-through of your fellow players and make notes on what the ball does. There was a time when the pins would tell you if you made a bad shot. Laughing at you would be the 5-7 or 8-10 (left-handers faced the 5-10 or the 7-9).

That era of stable back ends and substantive pins is long gone. Today's players have atomic bombs in their hands, dry back ends, and Tinker Toy pins. The environment is so conducive to high scoring that very rarely do the pins deliver such a message. About the only way to entice the pins to "talk" to us would be not to use a monster ball.

MISTAKE 36

The Wandering Syndrome

A common error, particularly among bowlers who lack confidence, is to be pocket-conscious with their shots. A far better approach is to be target-conscious. From the top of my swing until long after my follow-through has been executed, I allow my target to act as a lure to me. Throughout my entire delivery, my eyes are locked on it.

As far as I'm concerned, there's a curtain behind the arrows. I pretend that I can't see the pins or my ball reaction. All that I think about is making a good shot and hitting my target. If I miss, it will be because of a physical error, not because I out-think myself. By dropping that "curtain" behind the target on every shot, you will make far better shots.

This is one of those items that belongs in the easier-said-than-done category. At both the amateur and professional levels, on important shots many players try to steer the ball to the pocket. This causes a wide variance in follow-throughs, inconsistent deliveries, changes in speed, and a variety of hand releases.

Bowling is a mental game. It's not a reaction game like tennis, where you react to a ball that's hit toward you at 120 miles per hour. As a bowler, you must discipline yourself. Don't even look at the pins until your ball has crossed the target. If you can do that, you'll become a much better player. Try shutting your eyes just before you release the ball. Trust me, doing so will clean up the shot.

MISTAKE 37

Rearing up at the Line ✓

When I'm at my best, my release and follow-through are smooth. When I'm apprehensive, I may rear up at the foul line rather than stay down with my shot.

Coming up too soon will cause an inconsistent release coupled with a short slide. A lot of bad things could then happen. Of these, the worst is that you'll pull out of your shot with your thumb and your fingers exiting simultaneously. The ball is then pitched out onto the lane.

There are plenty of very good bowlers who rear up at the line, but they all do so after they've released the shot. Senior pro Gene Stus has a bad knee that often forces him to compete with some degree of discomfort. That pain can cause him to rear up prematurely. It's a battle he knows that he must fight if he's to be competitive.

Frayed nerves can lead to rearing up at the foul line.

MISTAKE 38

Bending from the Waist

Your knees should bend but your waist should not. The more your waist is bent, the shorter your slide will be, and you'll experience major problems with maintaining a consistent hand release.

The short slide, which is also caused by stepping on your rubber heel on the sliding foot, leads to the hand pulling back out of the ball. The fingers and thumb exit together, robbing you of accuracy and power. You'll lose continuation and follow-

Bend too much at the waist and you'll lose power.

through, and you have no chance to make a good shot without them.

Remind yourself to walk tall during your delivery until the gradual bending of the nonsliding knee begins your descent. Have the weight of your sliding foot supported by the balls under the toes, not your heel.

MISTAKE 39

Smelling Something Foul

There are a lot of reasons why you don't want to cross that thin black line. First, of course, is that a foul results in losing credit for any pins you might knock down on that shot. Also, you could go flying as your foot steps on a puddle of lane conditioner.

The obvious correction is to stand farther away from the line when you assume the address position. If that doesn't do it, during practice stand far closer to the line. Take little steps and pretend that there's a 10,000-foot cliff on the other side of the foul line and it has some very hungry alligators on the bottom.

Summary

All bowling lanes lead to the foul line. While you can get there any number of ways and still be successful, here are a few keys to include during your finish:

1. Remain well-balanced throughout the finish.
2. Bend from the knees, not from the waist.
3. Fill the hole during your slide.
4. Hold your follow-through pose without rearing up at the line.
5. Remember, all the proper technique in the world will be for naught if you don't stay behind that thin black line.

CHAPTER 6

Physical Adjustments

The legendary Sam Snead once observed that most golfers would starve to death if they gripped a knife and fork the way they gripped a golf club. In the same way, bowlers would be an endangered species if adjusting to surroundings was a prerequisite for survival. Compared to the majority of amateurs I've observed, the dinosaur was a master at adaptation.

Perhaps because all bowling lanes look the same, most people attempt to play them the same way. Just as a golfer selects a different club for a 440-yard par-4 than for a 145-yard par-3, you should employ a different strategy for playing an oily lane versus one that's dry. That's because for a shot to hook, there must be friction between the surface of the ball and the lane. The lane dressing (oil) eliminates or greatly decreases that friction and, with that, the amount of hook.

Proprietors apply the dressing to the front segment of the lane to help protect it and to comply with American Bowling Congress regulations. Because the lane's *heads* (front) are *wet* and the back ends are *dry*, a hook shot will go straight until it leaves the oil. At about the point where it "hits the dry," it should begin its arc toward the pocket. The distance from the pindeck at which this occurs is known as your *break point*.

The amount of oil and the length of the lane that it's applied on will influence both the amount that your shot hooks and the location of your break point. A ball that "goes long" (that is, rolls far down the lane before starting to hook) may never get into a powerful roll. As a result, the ball deflects away from the center of the lane after hitting the headpin. This leads to weak 10-pin leaves. It also causes pocket splits such as the 5-7 and 8-10 for a right-handed player or the 5-10 and 7-9 for a lefty.

Like his dad, Pete Weber is extremely versatile, which allows him to excel on all lane conditions. *Courtesy of the PBA*

Conversely, heads that are very dry can cause the ball to hook too soon. This makes being accurate extremely difficult. It's your challenge to find a way to get your ball through the head area before it begins to grip the lane. This is essential if your strike ball is to enter into the desired skid-roll-hook sequence.

Be aware that oil can be applied so as to make a lane as difficult as reading *War and Peace* in one day, or as easy as finding an annoying infomercial on late night TV. Because of the potential for mischief, the ABC regulates our sport. Otherwise, proprietors wishing to lure customers with false success could block their facility so as to send scores soaring.

A *block* occurs when the central boards are heavily oiled while the outside flanks are dry. This causes the ball to roll toward the pocket without, it is hoped, wandering through the nose. There are times when such a condition may be created due to a large number of players wearing a track area toward the pocket. However, at least in theory, the manner in which conditioner is initially applied shouldn't assist or hamper the bowler.

Theories, as we know too well, only rarely mirror reality. The truth is that owners of bowling centers understand that their customers are a lot happier after rolling a 220 than a 120. Since happy customers lead to ringing cash registers, it's in the industry's interest to provide a high-scoring environment. Add to that the great improvement in equipment, and it's little wonder that there has been a huge increase in the number of honor scores since a generation ago.

In the old days, everyone used a rubber bowling ball. To make adjustments required making physical changes. Now, switching balls can accomplish what a young Mike Durbin had to do by changing his line, ball speed, hand or wrist position, release, or some combination of the above. Sometimes it seems as if having talent is not as important as picking the right ball to match the condition.

But even with the growing importance of equipment, certain lane conditions demand physical versatility. To become a good player, you must learn how to execute different types of shots and how to recognize which will work best in a given situation.

You must also make an educated guess as to which strike line will work best. Complicating matters is that oil rarely stays in one place for very long, so the characteristics of a

Hall of Fame member Johnny Petraglia's heyday was spent rolling exclusively rubber balls. *Courtesy of the PBA*

lane will evolve with every shot. The phenomenon of bowling balls moving the oil toward the pins (making the heads more dry and the back end wetter) is known as *carrydown*. It becomes an especially acute challenge when several bowlers are playing the same part of the lane since the more balls that travel over that area, the more the dressing pattern will be altered.

Carrydown is the factor that's most responsible for those occasions when the world's greatest players are embarrassed by shooting a low score while competing in the title round of a televised professional tournament. There is a transition period during which the lane plays like the golf equivalent of a 660-yard par-5 in which the fairway is 10 yards wide. The only strategy at that point is to throw hard and straight and do a lot of praying (my football buddies would probably suggest punting).

In most cases at the amateur level, the lanes will be playable. Your challenge is to discover the combination of ball surface, hand release, shot speed, and line so as to obtain the break point and pocket entry angle that provide you with the greatest margin of error. A handful of pros generate so much power that they can "create area." Such is their talent that they can miss their target area by several boards and still strike.

While creating area is always a plus, an even greater factor is learning how to play in the most productive manner for a specific condition. The good news is that bowling centers tend to have characteristics. When I play in a league, it isn't long before I know the best way to play its lanes on most occasions. However—and this is key—there are differences based on the time of day you bowl (the later in the day, the more the lanes have been used and, thus, the more the oil has been moved from the original position); the lane you use (many of the houses that have two rows of lanes are almost like bowling in two different centers); if the person in charge of dressing the lane decides to alter the pattern (*never* bowl in a center in which the proprietor has just had a big fight with his or her spouse!); and even climate changes.

The ability to adjust becomes even more important if you bowl in more than one center on a regular basis, especially if you enter tournaments that require you to compete on a wide variety of conditions.

Regardless of your situation, it's imperative that you become both versatile and knowledgeable. Players who only play one way will rarely achieve success when the lanes don't suit their style. It's your challenge to be able to score well even when having to use what we pros refer to as our "B game."

You can make several technical adjustments. The most common of these involve changing your shot's speed by lofting it far down the lane or laying it short, and altering your strike line by moving your feet sideways on the approach or changing your target. And, of course, you can make equipment adjustments (see Chapter 7).

Unlike golfers who can see their hazards (ponds, sand traps, and woods), we bowlers must attempt to locate a transparent object (oil) by observing how our shot reacts to the lane. Moreover, you can only do so after having executed a shot correctly. It all comes down to trial and error. The quicker you're able to discover the right formula, the greater competitive edge you will gain.

MISTAKE 40

Taking the Proverbial "Three-Hour Tour"

Too many of us are like Gilligan, setting sail on a three-hour tour (to the lanes) but failing to keep track of where we are. Before you are cast away on the deserted island of low scoring, be certain to make a mental note of where you are before every shot.

To do so requires a quick reminder in lane "geography." There are 39 boards, each of which travels from the back of the approach to the pins. On every 5th board is painted a dot on the back, on the middle of the approach, and at the foul line. As you look down the lane, you will see an arrow painted on every 5th board.

If you were to draw a line from those dots to the seven visible pins (the 5 pin, 8 pin, and 9 pin are partially hidden behind other pins), each of your lines would intersect an arrow. A lane has seven arrows. The first arrow from the right channel is in line with the 10 pin, the second with the 6 pin, the third with the 3 pin, the center with the headpin, the fifth with the 2 pin, the sixth with the 4 pin, and the seventh with the 7 pin.

Every fifth board is home to dots, an arrow, and a pin.

For easy identification, the arrow that's the closest to the right channel is known as the first arrow to a right-handed player. The first arrow as defined by a southpaw is the one that's on the far left side of the lane.

Knowing your lane lingo is important because it provides you with an easy means of reference. For example, a right-handed bowler might declare that she is standing on 20 and playing 8. That means that her starting position on the approach has her left foot on top of the dot that's in the exact center of the lane. She is aiming her ball at the 8th board, which is between the first and second arrow. The pocket is on the 17th board.

The experienced player is careful to know exactly where he is positioned prior to each shot. This promotes a consistent means of aiming and it allows one to make positional adjustments.

MISTAKE 41

Not Moving from Side to Side

Bowling's most common adjustment is to alter one's strike line. Although this isn't a particularly difficult proposition, it's a step that relatively few players attempt.

Let's say that you have just made a good shot in which your timing felt right, your release was smooth, and your ball rolled over your target. However, the shot's results didn't meet your expectations. What to do?

Here's *the* golden rule of adjustments: Maintain the same target on the lane, but move your feet in the *same* direction as you missed. If the ball strayed to the left, move your feet to the left. If you missed to the right, move to the right.

Assuming that you're using the arrows (or an area near them) as your target, here's the formula. For every board that you move toward one side, the position where the ball should reach the pindeck is altered by one and a half boards in the opposite direction. Thus, a right-handed bowler whose shot was three boards right wants the next shot to finish three boards farther to the left. To do that, he should move his feet two boards to the right on the approach.

Bowling is a sport, not a science. This move should work. However, if the oil pattern is uneven, your shot could overreact or underreact. This would dictate a subsequent adjustment.

Here's an example. Your feet are on 20 and you're aiming at 10 (the second arrow). You execute properly, but your ball hits through the nose and you're facing a 4-6 split. Thus, your shot finished on the 20th board, which is three boards high. Dividing three by one and a half tells you that a two-board move is required. For your next shot, you stand on 22 (two boards to the left of the center of the approach). In theory, a good delivery should produce a strike.

The odds are that the above formula will bear fruit most of the time. However, on some occasions your ball may overreact to the lane. That's because your move changed the angle of your shot just enough that the ball left the central part of the lane that still had oil and strayed into a drier area. To stay in the so-called "oil line," make what's known as a two-and-one move. This adjustment involves moving your feet two boards and your target one board in the same direction (either both to the left or both to the right).

My tipoff that this adjustment is preferred to the normal "miss left–move left" strategy is that I've noticed that my ball has begun to hook way too soon. That would tell me that the heads have broken down. In that case, a two-and-one move is my first option or, in some cases, I might even move three-and-one. If that doesn't work, move another two-and-one or three-and-one. This will allow you to hit the pocket and, it's hoped, for your ball to slide through the front portion of the lane.

One consideration that can't be emphasized enough: *Never* adjust following a physical error that results in a poorly executed shot.

MISTAKE 42

Being a Blockhead

A *reverse* block is when the lane conditioner is a bowler's worst nightmare. It occurs when the center of the lane is dry and the outsides are wet. A ball shot wide enters what's known as an "out of bounds" area since once it touches that segment of the lane it has virtually no chance of reaching the pocket. But the dry central section makes it extremely tough to keep a shot on line.

This conspires to lead to low scoring. The rule that we pros employ: The lower the scores, the fewer the number of boards the shots should cross. Try the aim-and-flame strategy—stand to the right (left-handers stand to the left) with

Going up the boards (also known as "playing outside") requires more speed and less hook. It's often the strategy du jour on difficult lane conditions.

your target almost directly in line to the pocket. Now, throw hard and straight. You won't string many strikes, but you probably won't suffer from too many split leaves and difficult spare clusters.

The move to the outside allows the ball to start in the oil. Remember, some initial skid is desired. The ball should begin to roll and, at the end, hook mildly. The shot's entry angle into the pocket should provide sufficient inertia to avert pocket splits.

MISTAKE 43

Failing to Adjust Ball Speed

Speed control is a tremendous weapon. The master was Earl Anthony. During practice he had his wife use a stopwatch to time how long it took the shot to reach the pins from the time it left his hand. He would then attempt to roll at least 200 shots at that precise speed. Next, he'd increase it by a fraction of a second. By doing so he developed a built-in calculator that he could rely on in tournament play.

It never occurred to me to practice that way. But Earl thinks differently than the rest of us do. As far as I'm concerned, his approach was pure genius, which is yet another reason why I consider him to be the greatest performer in bowling history.

Earl's ability to fractionally alter his speed and then maintain that exact speed on subsequent shots was remarkable. His formula was to roll his shots more slowly when his strike ball didn't get back to the pocket and changing his line didn't bear fruit. This was common when the lanes tended to be slick.

The exact opposite, throwing harder, was used on drier lanes and when his normal shot didn't get back to the pocket even after having moved his feet. Probably no player was any better at adding a few miles per hour than Nelson Burton, Jr. That's because he grew up bowling on lacquer lanes in St. Louis where there was a definitive track shot. To keep the ball in that golden pathway to the pocket often required extra velocity.

MISTAKE 44

Changing Ball Speed with the Heave-Ho Method

Speed control is also important when you move on the approach. Playing up the boards usually dictates an increase in your shot's velocity. Playing deep inside usually calls for rolling the ball more slowly so that it can better grip the lane.

Any difference in ball speed should be accomplished without compromising good technique. You can throw the ball harder without losing your balance and without having to heave it down the lane. And you can slow it down without so babying the shot that you sacrifice a powerful roll.

The higher address position (right) will lengthen your armswing which, in turn, will generate greater ball speed.

To increase speed, hold the ball higher while in the address position. This will increase the length of your armswing and, with it, make for a higher backswing. Gravity's force will then pull the weight of the ball downward faster. Your alternative, the use of sheer force and muscle, may be needed when you wish to greatly increase your shot's velocity. One trick is to move your target farther down the lane and to concentrate on zipping through your follow-through.

I have two options when I need to decrease speed. If I'm throwing my strike shot reasonably straight, I simply concentrate on taking a little bit off my shot as I follow through. It's akin to a smooth swing in golf or try-ing to just meet the ball while batting in baseball. Your body should respond to what your mind dictates as long as that change isn't radical.

My alternative is to roll the ball a little bit forward in my hand so that the center of the ball is recessed toward my wrist. I combine this with a shortened armswing by holding the ball below waist height during the address. I come through the shot smoothly with my hand chasing the ball to cause a cupping action during the release. This decreases ball speed while also increasing the hook. For those of you who are familiar with his style, try to picture the way that veteran PBA star Bob Benoit bowls.

To learn the Benoit method, follow Bob's lead. He began his cupped wrist–slow speed learning process by practicing with a very light ball. As soon as he could control it, he gradually worked his way up until he felt comfortable bowling in that manner while using a 16-pound ball.

Increasing speed, especially on dry lanes, is one tactic for improving accu-racy on non–double-wood spare leaves (discussed in Chapter 8). How-ever—and this is important—you shouldn't throw the ball so hard that your balance and timing are compromised.

MISTAKE 45

Forgetting the Axiom About an Exception to Every Rule

Earlier we covered the rule of moving in the direction that you missed. But this can cause a problem in extreme circumstances. All of us should be able to perform outside of our comfort zones. However, too much movement may be counterproductive.

A bowler who relies on power may find it especially difficult to play up the boards via a far outside line. The bigger your hook and the revolutions you generate, the less likely it is that you'll want to stand on a lower-numbered board. Conversely, a finesse player like myself who doesn't generate many revs may find it especially difficult to carry while playing deep inside (for example, when a righty stands on the far left side of the approach).

Think of bowling as politics, with power players being Democrats and finesse players being Republicans. A Democrat is probably comfortable being anywhere from the far left to the middle. Those in the GOP are fine as long as they're anywhere from the middle to the far right. (Since I've invoked politics, I'll further confuse the issue by reversing the formula for left-handed players; thus a lefty power player becomes a Republican and a lefty finesse player becomes a Democrat.)

This doesn't mean that I can't play inside. A favorable oil line could allow me to remain sufficiently competitive that I could possibly still make the top 24 of a tournament, although I couldn't seriously challenge for a title that week. As a general principle, the more that I must move to the left, the farther down in the standings I will be.

Why, then, would I play to the left at all? Because my scores would be even lower if I insisted on staying in my comfort zone during periods in which lane conditions dictated moving. My only other option is to start the ball to the far right so that it begins its journey mired in oil. Because the back ends are so dry, the ball should finish strong. However, you

It's vital to be sufficiently versatile so as to be able to survive when lane conditions dictate playing deep inside.

had better be hair-splitting accurate because even a one-board miss on the front end of the lane could lead to disaster.

Nor am I implying that a power player can't aim up the boards. Appreciating how difficult it is for a bowler to compete while using his less-preferred option is another advertisement for Earl Anthony's brilliance. I saw him win some tournaments while bowling in the manner least favorable to his attributes.

Anthony's versatility is a quality that the truly great players possess. The two men who have best exemplified this talent in the 1990s are Walter Ray Williams and Norm Duke. Small wonder that they have excelled year in and year out despite changes in lane conditions and the type of ball that was in vogue at the time.

MISTAKE 46

Maintaining the Same Distance from the Foul Line

One of the first things youth bowlers are taught is their "natural starting point." The instructor will walk them to the foul line and have them face the settee area. They're then told to walk four and a half strides. They're told that where they end up is the distance they should stand from the foul line when beginning their deliveries.

Obviously, as one grows, the length of stride increases. Most adults use the majority of the approach. Some very tall pros will assume the address position with their heels hanging over the edge of the surface. Conversely, a short player will likely begin a lot closer to the foul line.

Even without knowing it, you have probably discovered what is your "natural" position. Mine is about 13 feet from the line. Knowing that allows me to make a different type of adjustment. Let's say that I'm leaving a lot of 10-pin spares. I can adjust my speed by rolling the ball slightly slower, or I can move three to four inches backward on the approach. This should cause my shot to land on the lane three or four inches sooner. In turn, the break point will be moved slightly farther from the pindeck so as to let the ball finish marginally higher in the pocket.

MISTAKE 47

Always Targeting the Arrows

Having arrows to aim at is very helpful. Don't take my word for it; just try moonlight bowling when the lights are low and you can't find an aiming point on the lane. But as useful as the arrows are, they aren't the only target that's available.

When your shots are hooking prematurely, an adjustment must be made. After your first shot creeped high, you moved slightly left (for a right-hander) or to the right (if you're a lefty). But that didn't provide the answer. Another option is to move your target farther down the lane.

Instead of looking at the second arrow, pick out a spot on the 10th board that is farther down the lane. This usually isn't as tricky as it sounds given that wood often has dark spots.

This should work because it will cause you to extend your armswing and follow-through. Moreover, it emphasizes concentration on your target which, in turn, helps to keep your head steady throughout your approach.

Conversely, you can move your target closer if you want to get your ball to enter into a roll sooner. This is desired when your shots won't get up to pocket and moving on the approach hasn't worked.

MISTAKE 48

Failing to Alter Wrist Positions

Even the most versatile players have strike lines that they prefer. We know that the amount your ball will hook can be altered by oil patterns. One choice is to change your strike line. Moving a few boards usually doesn't present much of a challenge.

But big changes make for big challenges. As mentioned, I can play deep inside if I must but I would far prefer not to do so. I can relegate that option to the last-resort strategy by first attempting to increase or decrease my shot's arc via other types of adjustments. One of these involves my wrist position. In this department you have a network of options—CBS (cupped, broken, or straight).

A cupped wrist creates more hook and more back end when the lanes are on the wet side or you're forced to play inside. It generates more revolutions on the ball to increase your power. Bowlers who rely on power tend to use it as their first option.

The straight/firm wrist is generally employed by most players when rolling on normal lane conditions. At the release point your fingers rotate from 6 o'clock to the 3 o'clock position (or from 6 o'clock to 9 o'clock for a left-handed player).

You can also bend your wrist backward. The so-called "broken wrist" release will retard your shot's hooking tendencies. It's used on dry lanes when you want your shots to go straighter. A by-product is an end-over-end roll, which helps the ball to produce a more predictable reaction, which, in turn, makes it easier to make the right adjustment more quickly. I use this a lot, especially when I'm playing the second arrow or to its right.

An additional advantage is that using the broken wrist makes it easy to repeat your delivery's techniques shot after shot. This duplication of movement increases your ability to be consistent.

MISTAKE 49

Never Taking the Subtle Approach

Those of us who are married know that there are times when a less obvious approach works best. I'm sure that Debbie Durbin will concur that I'm not always the most subtle individual. But, at least, I can be on the lanes.

I use a fingertip grip. In theory, that means that my fingers enter the ball up to the first joint. There are times when I bury my fingers deep inside my ball. This is a way to get more lift and turn during my release so as to generate additional power and hooking action to my shots.

There are other times when I'm fighting to find the right feel. I sometimes will back my fingers out a little bit, which will help create a cleaner and more relaxed release.

A clean exit of the thumb prior to the fingers is essential on a strike shot delivery. What to do when your thumb is hanging ever so slightly in that hole but you can sense that removing a piece of bowling tape from the hole would cause the ball to slip out of your hand? My tactic is to have my thumb in the ball about one-eighth of an inch less. This gets it out of the ball slightly earlier and, even more importantly, with a clean exit.

Angling the feet away from the target is another trick of the trade. When I aspire to get the ball farther down the lane without having to move sideways, I turn my toes slightly inward on the approach (thus, a right-hander's feet point to the left while a left-hander's feet point to the right). The first step will wander slightly in that direction, which, in turn, will help the shot to go farther down lane. You'll find that the shot will get through the head portion of the lane a bit farther. Turning your feet to the right (for a right-handed player) will force you to walk to your target when you're playing inside.

To delay a shot's break point, direct your toes slightly away from your bowling hand.

MISTAKE 50

Being Closed-Minded

Far too many players inadvertently limit themselves because they lack the initiative to experiment. Your mind should be as flexible as a gymnast's body so that you don't lock yourself into a rigid compartment. If you convince yourself that you can bowl only one way, you will always be limited in what you can achieve.

Watching a truly great bowler adjust to varying conditions allows those with an educated eye to appreciate the talent of that individual. PBA Hall of Famer David Ozio is known as "The Wizard." It's not because his surname starts with "Oz;" it's because he's done some remarkable things on lanes that nobody else could hope to match.

Dave often competes head to head in challenge matches. By the time he's hit the lanes, there's less oil than after the OPEC-imposed shortage of the 1970s. So dry is the lane that even the hardest shell ball hooks like crazy. I've seen Dave place his fingers across the holes with only his thumb in the ball and proceed to toss his shot dead straight at a time when foes can barely keep their shots on the lane. Yes, that's talent. But it also demands an incredible amount of practice so as to have mastered several techniques. And it must be accompanied by an assertive "can do" personality.

Credit an open mind and a wide range of skills with helping David Ozio earn 1991 Player of the Year recognition.
Courtesy of the PBA

Trust yourself to try these different things. Before attempting a new strategy, Norm Duke likes to visualize it with his mind's eye painting a perfect picture that includes the desired result. He insists that being creative is a key to his success.

Summary

We all play at different levels. Professional bowlers try things that most others might not even imagine. Perhaps being creative to the typical bowler is simply to move left and to play the third arrow when the lane is screaming at everyone to move inside but most everyone else is afraid to try (or doesn't even know that to be an option). Whatever your level, don't be a tenpin T-rex. Adjust, adapt, and prosper.

CHAPTER 7

Equipment

The wide range of bowling paraphernalia on the market all boils down to one common purpose: to help you perform your best. Some pieces of equipment are preventive in nature, such as resin bags, which help to dry your hand to keep the ball from slipping off your fingers. Others offer augmentation. This category includes wrist devices that can provide the optimum position for your hand so as to increase (or decrease) the amount of hook that you impart on each shot.

There are only two items you must use: a bowling ball and shoes. Making educated decisions, especially when it comes to selecting which ball to throw, is vital. In addition, a ball's characteristics can be altered either by applying sandpaper or by using a polishing machine. The latter provided me with an investment opportunity that any Wall Street tycoon would envy; in 1972 I spent 75 cents and my return was approximately $50,000.

Due to my full-time job commitment at Bainbridge Colonial Lanes in my hometown of Chagrin Falls, Ohio, I had entered only three Win-

At the end of the day, little things can spell the difference between success and failure. *Courtesy of the PBA*

ter Tour events that year. As such, that chapter of the Tournament of Champions would be the last for which I was eligible. The only way to earn a ticket to subsequent editions of bowling's most prestigious event would be to gain the seven-year exemption that goes to the winner.

I came roaring out of the gate and was 440 pins over par after the first eight-game block. I added another 368 sticks in the next round. My white-hot White Dot ball had produced a 250+ average for those 16 games, which had me comfortably in front of the pack.

Although I subsequently cooled off considerably, I spent most of the remainder of that week either leading or running a close second to Tim Harahan. But in the position round match, I rolled a dismal 147 to drop behind Larry Laub and into the third-seed position for the title round.

I arrived at the lanes early the next morning, fully intent on experimenting so as to rediscover my lost touch. I tried a wide variety of hand/wrist position adjustments. Hitting the pocket wasn't a problem, but I just couldn't carry all 10 pins with anything less than an absolutely flawless delivery. Experimenting with a different ball did little to change my bleak outlook. From experience, I knew all too well that without a decent margin for error I would be doomed.

About a half-hour before the telecast was to begin, Columbia salesman Bernie Wise offered a suggestion. Since nothing else was working, why not spend 50 cents and put my ball in the Lustre King machine for five minutes? I can distinctly recall thinking to myself, "Why not, I've got nothing to lose."

All of a sudden, my "new" ball was shattering the pins. If I threw it out to the right, it came roaring back like a freight train chugging downhill. If I pulled it slightly, the ball would hook to the 17th board and, as if pulled by an invisible magnet, veer straight ahead to rip through the rack.

I had gone from having little hope to believing that there was no way that Harahan, Teata Semiz, or future Hall of Famers Laub or George Pappas could beat me as long as I didn't beat myself.

My only concern was that the wax that represented my magic formula might wear off. Five minutes before air time I again gave the ball to Bernie for a 25-cent (two-minute) spin in the machine. I barely got it back in time to roll a few more practice shots.

In the opening match Pappas defeated Semiz, 268–248. Despite the astronomical scores, I remained fully confident. George slumped to a 226 in game two as I won easily by shooting a 248. I began with a string of strikes to overwhelm Laub, 269–224. After chopping the 6 pin off the 10 pin in the first frame of the title game, I produced an eight-bagger to defeat Harahan, 258–187.

It's hard to say precisely how much that victory meant to me in additional endorsements and appearances. I do know this—first prize was worth $25,000. The chance to enter the next seven Tournament of Champions allowed me to finish second in 1977, and the official take in that event over the span of the exemption added another $23,825 to my kids' college education fund. On top of that were several thousand dollars more in squad bonus payments for high games.

And to imagine that I went from having virtually no shot to dominating because of spending 75 cents. Even better, it was Bernie's three quarters and I never did pay him back. I can only hope that he'll settle for his original investment and not demand the entire payoff!

To be honest, I'm not sure if that formula would work today. I suspect that a ball polishing machine isn't meant to be compatible with reactive balls. Nowadays, players use a fine sandpaper to make the ball smoother so as to hook earlier. A rough grit paper is used to get the ball to better grip an oily lane. It's the equivalent of placing chains on a car's tires to grip a road more effectively.

Regardless of which option works best in a situation, the lesson is the same. Knowledge of your equipment options coupled with a willingness to experiment intelligently can provide you with a great competitive advantage. Having the right ball in your hand is often the difference between winning on the Pro Tour versus fighting to just grind out a check. We'll deal with bowling ball options later in this chapter.

Smart players subscribe to the old Boy Scout motto of always being prepared. Unfortunately, the bags of many participants are missing items that can make a major difference in the ability to perform.

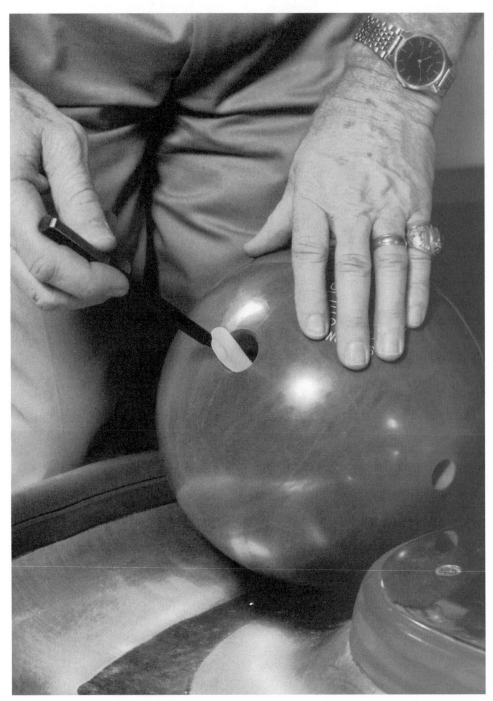

A common sight at PBA and LPBT tournaments—a pro adding or removing thumb-hole tape.

MISTAKE 51

Failing to Use Tape

One of the most significant intangibles in bowling is feel. Without your hand being relaxed while gripping the ball, you cannot execute properly on a consistent basis. Using special bowling tape to alter the size of one's thumb hole allows that ball to fit like the proverbial glove.

It's virtually impossible for me to communicate why sometimes my hand sits comfortably inside my ball and other times my grip seems as awkward as a blind date. In some ways bowling feel is reminiscent of Supreme Court Justice Potter Stewart's written opinion in the landmark case of Jacobellis vs. Ohio. Justice Stewart declared that he couldn't define pornography but that he knew it when he saw it. Likewise, I can't say why a ball feels right, but I definitely know it when I feel it.

And I do know what I can do when a good feel is absent. That calls for adding or removing a piece (or two) of tape from my thumb hole. That's because as you bowl your thumb's size changes. Depending on the weather (especially the humidity) and your body makeup, your thumb could enlarge or shrink after several games. Not accommodating that change by making a commensurate change in the size of your thumb hole by adding or removing tape is as silly as someone with size seven feet attempting to jog while wearing size nine running shoes.

The special bowler's tape that you can buy in any good pro shop is usually inserted into the back of the thumb hole between the 6 o'clock and 8 o'clock positions (a left-handed player typically places it between 6 o'clock and 4 o'clock). Doing so allows the tape to touch only the back of your thumb (the part that's located under your fingernail). This allows you to feel the surface of the ball on the pad of your thumb.

Many bowlers use a cork insert to help achieve a smoother release. Peel the tape off the back and place it into the front of the thumb hole to improve your feel. When making an

A cork insert.

adjustment, senior pro Larry Laub removes the cork grip and puts the sticky part of the tape facing out. He then puts it back into the front of his thumb hole. Doing so allows him to add a piece of tape to make the fit more snug while maintaining the same feel.

My preference is to put the tape in both the front and the back of my thumb hole. My routine calls for removing the old tape, sanding the inside of the hole, and then putting back as many new pieces as I estimate are needed. In some ways, it's not unlike a sweaty tennis player who puts on a fresh shirt during a changeover. For some reason, one feels instantly refreshed.

Knowing that you have a good feel should provide you with a psychological edge. After all, if you don't think you can throw that strike, generally, you can't. A ball that doesn't feel comfortable in your hand puts a doubt in your mind that you will execute properly. Bowling is sufficiently challenging without making it even more so by negatively influencing your confidence.

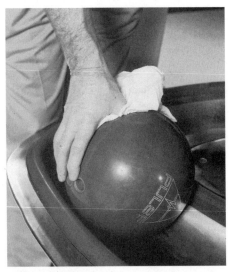

By wrapping your thumb in tissue and inserting it briefly into the ball, you will obtain a cleaner release than had you attempted to deliver a shot when your thumb hole felt snug.

MISTAKE 52

Throwing a Shot When the Thumb Hole Is Snug

There are times when your thumb feels as tight as a pair of jeans after eating a five-course meal. This is especially problematic if no tape remains that you could remove. What to do?

A trick that we pros employ is to wrap one's thumb with a facial tissue. We then jam it into the hole and remove it after a second or two. This causes the thumb to sufficiently shrink so as to fit comfortably for the upcoming shot.

MISTAKE 53

Neglecting to Take Advantage of Wrist Devices

The secret to an effective strike shot is imparting a roll on the ball that powers through the pins like the proverbial knife through butter. By cupping (flexing) your wrist you will markedly improve your ability to carry those half-hits. Tinkering with the angle at which your wrist is positioned will alter the amount of revolutions on your shot as well as how much (and when) it hooks.

In the early 1980s I had myself videotaped while bowling. By studying those tapes in slow motion I discovered that my wrist was only slightly bent at the point of release (after my thumb had already exited but while my fingers were still in the ball). Try as I might, I couldn't fully cock my wrist while retaining a natural feel. No matter how much I experimented, I couldn't get enough snap on the ball to match the big guns strike for strike.

It was clear that the problem was my inability to get my wrist into a stronger position. But what years of practice couldn't accomplish, spending $25 achieved. By wearing a wrist device I was able to cup the ball with ease. I have worn one ever since.

Although I was born in 1941, I now throw a more powerful strike ball than I did during my heyday several decades ago. Does that mean that I always wear a wrist aid? Of course not. There are lane conditions in which my angle and a dry back end provide me with more than enough snap. Adding to that wouldn't improve my carry and might compromise my accuracy. So when I want my shots to go straighter, I go natural or I use an aid that provides support while maintaining a relatively flat angle.

A wrist device can increase power while also alleviating stress on your wrist.

There are times when I can change the way that I'm playing the lane merely by switching which wrist device I'm using. A few years ago I led a PBA event in Tucson by some 250 pins. That particular center had a split personality; the difference between the low end of that house and the high side was almost like bowling in two entirely different establishments. Most of my rivals struggled on at least one of those conditions, but I thrived on both.

I was successful because I determined early on that at one end I wanted my shots to hook more while on the other end I wanted my strike ball to roll far straighter. While others switched balls, tinkered with their shot speed, or experimented with a different strike line, I merely changed my wrist device.

By not changing balls, I kept the same feel. By maintaining the same strike line I had little trouble adjusting from lane to lane. My performance that week underscored an important principle in the modern game: Sometimes the equipment you decide to use is even more important than your ability.

MISTAKE 54

Exercising False Economy When Buying Footwear

To save money, you can always purchase a pair of inexpensive bowling shoes at a discount store. But you'll get what you pay for. What you save in dollars you will sacrifice in both comfort and durability.

As you're probably aware, the bottoms of your two shoes are different. A right-handed bowler will have leather on the bottom of the left shoe so as to help her slide. The right sole will consist of rubber to act as a brake.

But how much you wish to slide can depend on your personal style as well as the condition of the lane's approach. Some surfaces tend to be as tacky as a velvet Elvis painting. Others are as slippery as a politician's election-year tax cut pledge. That's why most pros own at least three pairs of shoes. As I write this, one company, Dexter, even makes a shoe that features an interchangeable sole.

As a general rule, high humidity will make the approach sticky. Bowling in a cold climate in winter in which the heater is blasting usually results in low humidity, which tends to make the approach more slippery. One of the trickier situations is when parts of the same approach are slippery and others are tacky. This is a common occurrence on synthetic surfaces.

My biggest footwear nightmare occurred while competing in Denver in a complex that featured artificial surface lanes coupled with a swimming pool. The pool's humidity made the approaches very sticky. Yet there were slippery patches.

One trick I discovered is to use cork inserts. Their teflon-like substance, when inserted into holes, allows the hand to clear the ball more quickly. I also peel one off and place it on the heel of my sliding shoe. That counteracts the friction on an overly sticky lane.

The lesser-used sides of the approaches of synthetic lanes tend to be stickier. Thus, you may stop short when attempting a cross-lane spare. My advice—be prepared. Before shooting that corner pin, move to the spot at the line at which you'll slide. Run your foot over that spot several times until you're satisfied that it's safe. Or, as pro bowler Jim Johnson is wont to do, place a sock over your sliding shoe.

Shoes, which are themselves an accessory, now come with accessories. Most manufacturers offer a conditioner that can be dabbed on the sole to promote sliding. This is an especially handy product for those of you who bowl in areas with high humidity. Another item is shoe guards. After bowling, you put your footwear into these bag-like covers, which protect against the possibility of a foreign substance clinging to the bottoms. You can also wear them over your shoes when strolling to the snack bar or the lounge to prevent stepping directly in a spill.

There's no way that you'll stick on the approach if you wear a sock on the outside of your sliding shoe.

MISTAKE 55

Neglecting Your Hand

A bowler's hand is as important as a carpenter's tools. It should be treated accordingly. The more games you roll, the greater the beating that your hand will take. Take this to the bank: No pro bowler will ever be asked to endorse a hand cream product!

It's not uncommon to see us pros dabbing our hands with a substance in much the same manner as one would apply nail polish. Skin-care products with nylon patches are used to cover over abrasions and blisters. You apply the liquid on the injured area, put the patch over it, then place more of the liquid over the patch. Either place your hand over the air blower or blow on it until it dries (which usually takes less than one minute).

These products can also be used as a preventive measure by applying them to vulnerable spots on your hand so as to avoid injuries. Either way, having it in your bag is a must if you plan on competing in events in which bowling a large number of games is required.

Your hand also needs to be dry (see Chapter 1 on the pre-shot routine). That means your bag should hold a towel and a resin bag. Most players

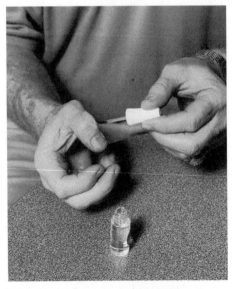

Don't wait until the damage has been done to take care of your most important tool.

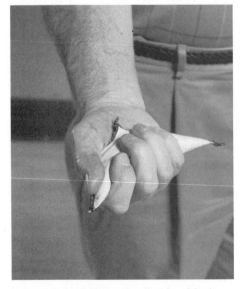

Make certain that your bowling hand is dry before shooting.

use the resin bag to dry only their hands, but former PBA star Steve Cook and others would tap it over the thumb hole. Steve, who is a massive 6'7", would then spin the ball in one hand while holding a towel in the other. In his hands a bowling ball looked more like a marble. His routine allowed him to obtain a better feel inside the ball.

There is also a large ultra-dry ball product. It looks like a huge resin bag and it fits in the palm of your hand like a ball. While it has a different feel than resin, it also helps to keep your hand moisture-free for a clean release.

MISTAKE 56

Not Taking Advantage of Grips

There are three methods of drilling finger holes: the conventional grip, the fingertip grip, and the semi-fingertip grip.

The conventional grip is usually used by beginners and involves fully inserting one's middle and ring fingers into the holes. It provides extra control, but at the expense of generating a powerful roll. The fingertip grip,

The conventional grip (left) and the fingertip grip (right).

in which the two fingers are inserted up to the first knuckle, is by far the preferred option of high-average players. It maximizes lift so as to improve the ball's roll. The semi-fingertip grip requires inserting your fingers between the first and second knuckles. However, without a joint to position precisely inside of the holes, it is very much a hit-or-miss proposition. Only a small handful of pros have used it, and I don't recommend it.

For the fingertip grip, more and more players are having their local pro shops install finger inserts. These plastic grips increase traction like a tire's tread, causing your fingers to stay in the holes a bit longer to improve your lift. Moreover, I find that the grips provide me with a more consistent and comfortable feel.

There are several different varieties. Some are oval; some are rounded. Some are soft; others are hard. Some even have ridges. All are good and each slightly alters your shot. Mostly, it's a matter of individual preference. Consult your local pro shop proprietor about the option that's best for you.

However, a word of warning is in order, especially for those of you who have a history of wrist injuries. Because your hand will remain in the ball longer, your fingers will be lifting an object that weighs up to 16 pounds. As such, finger grips can strain tendons.

The first few times you bowl with grips, roll your shots smoothly and with less speed. Allow your body to progress gradually as it becomes accustomed to the new equipment.

MISTAKE 57

Poor Ball Selection

Choosing the right bowling ball has become a vital element of success in the PBA and on the LPBT. There are so many good players that the competitive edge often goes to the bowler who selects the ball that provides the greatest margin for error.

That aspect of the sport is a relatively new phenomenon. When I made my Tour debut in 1967, I used the same Ebonite Gyro my entire rookie year. That black rubber ball with a pancake weight block was used for every strike shot and each spare conversion attempt.

In the 1970s, Don Johnson had great success using a plastic ball. The plastic balls rolled differently than rubber balls. They slid more on oil, and when they reached the dry back end of the lane they hooked more dramatically (the rubber balls made a more even arch). Unless a player had fingers of steel, which I never did, rubber balls required traction in order to hook.

As Johnson became a dominant player, plastic balls became the rage. The 1980s were subsequently dominated by urethane balls. As I write this, the various versions of reactive resin balls are now the weapon of choice.

So effective are the reactive resins that when they were first introduced, many players referred to them as "cheater balls." As the name implies, they react violently to what is on the lane. If the surface is very oily, they will slide forever. Should the lane be dry, however, they'll hook like crazy. Get them within a zip code or two of the pocket and they will shatter pins. But—and here's the big drawback—their tendency to overreact can lead to some very ugly split combinations.

The urethane balls of the 1980s came in two-piece and three-piece varieties. Each had a core and a shell, with the three-piece also featuring an internal weight block. By drilling the ball slightly off center, one side could weigh more than the opposite side. That dense material weighs more than the cover stock. It can be positioned to create what's known as side weight. The block can be altered to feature finger weight or thumb weight. And you can have top weight or bottom weight.

American Bowling Congress rules place a limit of one ounce of side and thumb or finger weight. No more than three ounces of top or bottom weight is permissible. Having more weight to the ball's outside, fingers, and top is known as *positive weights* that will increase your hook. Conversely, *negative weights* to the ball's bottom and thumb will delay your shot's break point and retard the hook. The manner in which you tend to roll your shots and the lane conditions upon which you most often compete are the factors that your pro will consider while trying to devise a formula that's best for you.

Most league bowlers on a typical house condition will want some finger, side, and top weight. The reason is that the combination of positive weights will make the ball skid long and hook later so as to hit the pins harder. The only way that this formula will get you in trouble is if the lanes are heavily oiled. On that condition the ball might not ever get into a roll and will skid down the lane like tires that are hydroplaning on a wet road. However, it's very rare when a house condition is of that variety.

On the other hand, tournament conditions can be slick. That's why the competitive player needs a more varied arsenal. Serious tournament players often carry four or five balls. As I'm sure you can guess, this can become a very expensive proposition.

Bowling balls are like computers; it seems that every year something new hits the market that renders its predecessors obsolete. There are literally hundreds of types of balls on today's shelves. By altering their weight blocks and surfaces, each one's characteristics can be modified. As such, you have countless options.

Only pros and the most serious of amateurs can expect to be aware of what's out there. The name of the game is to carry those off-hits, and the appropriate ball that's drilled just right for your game can make a major difference. I encourage you to seek out a highly respected pro in your area from whom to purchase your next ball.

It only looks as if most of us pros are packed for a European holiday. Having several ball options is so vital on the Tour that double-size bowling bags on wheels have become a necessity.

Or should I say *balls*. Serious players take two double bags to the lanes. At the least, you need more than one ball. You should have a strike ball that's designed to excel on oily lanes and another that's meant to thrive on a dry surface. And you should have a spare ball whose hard surface helps it to go straight.

I recommend that one of your balls have a porous cover stock. This will allow it to "bite" the lane even when it's slick. A good counterpoint is a ball that will go long and hook late for when the lanes are dry. A reactive resin ball with a smooth or polished cover stock fits this bill. If you're sufficiently serious and willing to shell out the money for a third strike ball, I would add a regular three-piece urethane ball. It will provide you with an even arc toward the pocket.

All players should own a spare ball that goes dead straight. A hard shell does the trick. So would a rubber ball, if you can still find one on the shelves. This ball is used for all spares in which double wood isn't involved.

All should be drilled to similar specifications. No two balls can be drilled to feature an identical grip. But the fewer the differences, the easier it is when you have to switch balls.

Just how important is matching the right ball to the lane condition on which you're competing? In my case, it meant the difference between breaking one of bowling's longest-standing records or falling short.

With two weeks remaining in the 1971–72 season, my average in the Friday Night Classic League at Bainbridge was just shy of the 238 mark that had been established by Walter "Skang" Mecurio in the Tomasch All-Star League in 1934–35. I needed at least one 800 series to erase his name from the record book.

In the first frame I left a weak 10 pin. Keith "Doc" Smith, the brother of bowling great Harry, smiled at me and declared, "You're in trouble already!" I thought I'd quieted my critic with a turkey, then left another weak 10 in the fifth. "Now you're really in trouble," he asserted. After a four-bagger I needed to strike out in the tenth to shoot a 268. But yet another half-hit 10 pin refused to fall. My final score was a most respectable 248.

From that point on, nothing stood. Twenty-four frames and 24 strikes later I had produced the only back-to-back perfect games of my career and a personal best 848 series. I felt like Ted Williams chasing the .400 mark in 1941. I knew that I could sit out the last day of the season and the record would be mine. Or, if I did bowl, a 709 was required.

Mr. Williams, as you may recall, decided to play based on the admirable belief that there would be no real honor in breaking a record while sitting on one's rear end. He showed his greatness on the last day of the season and ended the year at .406. My choice was far more simple since my team was barely holding on to first place in a 12-team circuit. They needed me to help them win.

In the week leading up to that night, a swarm of American Bowling Congress officials came down to check the lanes to make certain that everything was kosher. At that time the rules were arbitrary; the oil had to be equal from gutter to gutter. That's a far cry from today's regulations, which allow a center to create a high-scoring condition by placing extra oil down the center of the lane.

However, proprietor Ray Arnold had enough experience to know that he could meet ABC's requirements while still giving this player every chance to break the record. Ray put down a block and then ran the machine over the lane to flood oil from gutter to gutter.

Once the lane was approved, I went down to the pair on which I was scheduled to compete that night. For two straight hours I rolled shot after shot through the track area. Doing so wore away the excess oil and created a path on which I would play that night. But you know about the saying about the best-laid plans.

I had planned to use the same ball with which I'd won the Tournament of Champions just three weeks prior. My back-up strategy called for a brand-new Columbia White Dot that I had yet to throw.

For my first warm-up shot, I stood on the 20th board and aimed at the second arrow. The result was a nose hit that left the 4-6 split. Not to worry, a simple adjustment was all that was needed. So I moved my feet two boards to the left. That shot hooked early and again the 4-6 remained. I moved another board to my left. This time it stayed wide and left the 2-4-5 cluster. Like a neon sign on my forehead, "No area!" flashed through my brain.

I felt like a boxer who expected to face a trial horse only to look across the ring and see Oscar De La Hoya staring him down. Before complete panic ensued, I grabbed the brand-new ball and moved over to the right lane. Standing on board 18, I looked at 10 (the second arrow). My shot went flush into the pocket and sent the pins flying. For my final practice toss, I repeated it on the left lane. Over the microphone came those words that we all know by heart, "Bowlers, please hold up on your practice."

I started out with the first six strikes. After that, I ground out a 739 and broke the record with 30 pins left over. Of even greater satisfaction was knowing that the next highest series in my league that night was a 610 (luckily, nobody drowned in all of the oil that Mr. Arnold had used to flood the lanes).

The reason for my success was that my new ball went farther down the lane before starting to hook and it covered fewer boards than the older ball whose track bit the lane. By getting through the head area I averted a disaster. I firmly believe that without switching balls, I would have been lucky to have shot even a 600. There's little doubt that I wouldn't have been able to come close to breaking the record.

Not all adjustments involve using a ball with a different surface. You can also use the Jenny Craig theory of tenpin; try losing some (ball) weight.

Legally, a bowling ball may not exceed 16 pounds. I've often heard it said that the ball's weight should be about 10 percent of that of the player who is using it. But my advice differs; I suggest using as heavy a ball as you can comfortably throw. When I worked at Riviera Lanes, my assistant manager was just over 5' tall and had a petite build. Yet, Stacy Childers has no problem handling a 15-pound ball, and her credits include having produced a sanctioned perfect game.

Despite towering over Stacy (I'm 6' 1"), we both use the same ball weight. I was in my early 50s when I made the change from a 16- to a 15-pound ball. And by the time I'm in my 60s, I expect to probably drop to 14 pounds when this ball starts feeling heavy.

Many senior citizens stubbornly refuse to make that adjustment. I find that the 15 is a lot easier on this body. The traditional disadvantage of a lighter ball was that it would tend to deflect more when hitting the pins so that carry was sacrificed. But today's balls are so efficient that I haven't suffered at all in that regard.

The lighter ball gives me more control. I don't tire as rapidly as I would with a heavier ball (a one-pound difference doesn't sound like much until you multiply it by the total number of shots that you execute in a given night or during a tournament). There is less wear and tear to my hand. In short, it has made the game more enjoyable for me.

There's no point in being macho or letting false pride overcome your common sense. Having fewer aches and pains makes it worth it. Besides, nobody who is watching can tell the difference.

MISTAKE 58

Reluctance to Change

Assuming you do have several balls at your disposal and that each serves a different purpose, there will be situations in which your inability to carry dictates considering a ball change. I can distinctly remember being faced with such a situation during the 1981 Miller High Life Open. I had qualified third for the televised title round that week at Red Carpet Lanes. During warm-ups I used both my LT-48 (rubber) and a plastic ball. Both were working well. My decision was to pick the ball that seemed to give me the better reaction.

I knew that I had to make a definitive choice. Oddly enough, a bit of Scripture crossed my mind from the book of James that declares that a double-minded man is unstable in all of his ways (James 1:8). So I opted to take a firm course of action and throw my plastic ball. I then put the other into my bag.

In my first match against Kevin Gillette, my opponent got a Brooklyn strike. I left the baby split (2-10). Right then and there I switched back to the rubber ball. I can't honestly say what made me do so after having "definitively" decided to use the plastic one. All I know is that my instinct proved correct as I proceeded to produce about a 790 series using the rubber ball, including a 277–165 title game win over the great Earl Anthony. The margin of that win remains a PBA title game record, a fact I've been known to remind Earl of from time to time.

So the lesson is to make a decision and stick with it. Unless, of course, you wish to pull a Durbin by abandoning your prior resolute decision so as to make another resolute decision!

MISTAKE 59

Failing to Stay Clean

The market is filled with new items, including a reactive ball cleaning system that is purported to remove all dirt and residue from the surface. "Standard" bowling balls (urethane, plastic, or rubber) tend to displace the oil on the lane, taking it from the front section and moving it to the back end closer to the pindeck. Known as carry-down, this can create strategic problems for players (for tips on combating that phenomenon, review the previous chapter).

However, reactives are different. They tend to "eat" the oil. This makes the track area quite dry, which is why after a bit of play has occurred these balls may start to hook way too soon and much too dramatically. This may call for lofting the ball or moving to a part of the lane where there is still front-end oil.

But it also calls for getting that oil off the surface and the pores of your ball. Failure to do so will allow a foreign substance—the oil—to be sandwiched between the lane and the surface of your ball. By eliminating the ball–lane friction you will be unable to exploit the full force of reactive action.

Sure, he's extremely talented and composed, but Dave Husted would never have been able to capture back-to-back (1995-96) U.S. Open crowns without being fully aware of how to best exploit his equipment options.
Courtesy of the PBA

The solution is a two-spray system. The first bottle is sprayed onto the track of the ball and then wiped off with a special towel-like scuff mitt. It's like a mitten that you wear on one hand while spinning the ball over it with the other. The second spray is then applied so as to fully restore the ball's tackiness.

I recommend that the typical league player who rolls under 10 games per week should do this once a month. We pros could do it after every block. The more you want your ball to bite the lane, the more important it is to do this regularly. With experience, you should be able to judge when a cleaning is required simply by observing the buildup on the track area of your ball.

MISTAKE 60

Why Carry the Weight of the World on Your Shoulders?

Being an NFL running back for several seasons is tough work. So one would think that Leroy Hoard wouldn't find the physical demands of bowling to be problematic after having been gang-tackled by Dallas or Miami. But after trying his luck in the 1996 Comfort Inn Classic in Sunrise, Florida, he said he ached all over.

Aside from having a hand that felt like it had been stepped on, Leroy admitted that he wasn't too fond of having to lug two bowling bags—each with two balls weighing a total of 32 pounds—from one end of the center to the other between games.

From personal experience, I have to concur. Under any circumstance, those bags are heavy, but they seem even heavier when your scores aren't what you want them to be!

The answer is to buy the new style of bag that resembles luggage you see at airports with a long pull-out handle and wheels. It's a lot easier to roll a bag that weighs around 35 pounds than it is to place that strap over your shoulder.

For those of us who bowl in wintry climates, there's also a safety issue. I've seen some bowlers take nasty spills in an icy parking lot that were made far worse by landing awkwardly under the weight of all of that equipment.

Aside from wheels and a retractable handle, a double-ball bag should have a separate compartment for your shoes. A good pair of bowling shoes isn't cheap, so why just throw them into the bottom of a bag where they'll be crushed by your balls?

MISTAKE 61

Not Being Ready to Flash a Blade

I always carry a knife in my bag. This decision has nothing to do with Earl Anthony being such a ferocious competitor! Rather, it's so that I can bevel the edges of the holes in the ball. Doing so allowed me to end a seven-year winless streak in 1979.

That week the Tour was in Syracuse and yours truly was again just grinding out a check while presenting no threat whatsoever to the leaders. I had been playing at or left of the third arrow all week long, which was certainly not my preferred line but the only one in which I had even a little luck that week at Holiday Bowl.

With two games remaining in qualifying rounds, I moved from one of that facility's three bays that consisted of 16 lanes apiece to a different set. I was lucky to have arrived just before the players on my new pair had finished bowling. One of them was completing a big game. I noticed that he was playing the second arrow. Since I was struggling, I thought to myself, "Why not?!" I then shot a 268 followed by a 279. I snuck into 22nd place for the 24-player match-play segment. I continued the hot streak the next three blocks to qualify in second place, including two wins on Friday night over the great Mark Roth.

On Saturday afternoon I was to roll on national television. That morning I noticed that my plastic ball looked like a heavyweight who had sparred a few too many rounds with Muhammad Ali. The finger holes were breaking and the front edges had become sharp. I wasn't about to discard a ball that had performed so well for me if I could help it. The solution was to use a bevel knife to carve away just enough of the edges so as to again make the edges of the holes smooth. I had to repeat that procedure a few times between shots on television, but it paid dividends as I again upset Roth and got the best of Alvin Lou to win the Syracuse Open. (A footnote—to appreciate how much sports have changed since then, my champion's paycheck was all of $8,000!)

One word of caution—you ought not to use a bevel knife on holes in which there are grips. The slight enlarging of the hole would take away the snug fit that's essential to add lift to your shot. However, I still use that knife on occasion, especially when I'm having problems with my thumb not exiting the ball cleanly. By removing some of the front part of the thumb hole I almost always clear the ball better on subsequent shots.

You can buy a bevel knife at your local hardware store or you can order from most pro shops a similar screwdriver-like tool that features a carbide steel blade. I can't guarantee you a PBA Tournament win, although I am certain that you'll find it useful. But just don't think that it will protect you from Earl in the tenth frame!

Summary

To knife through the scoresheet, you must have equipment that works for you. I recommend finding a knowledgeable pro shop operator who carries equipment within your budget constraints, who can customize a ball (or balls) that are compatible with your needs.

After acquiring a good pair of shoes, make certain that your bowling bag is stocked with a resin bag, a wire bush, a bowling towel, facial tissues, and bowling tape. Optional items include a wrist device, cork inserts, shoe-surface conditioners, a ball spray system, a bevel knife, a skin-care product such as nylon patches, and, yes, a few quarters for the ball polishing machine just in case you find yourself competing in the Tournament of Champions.

CHAPTER 8

Converting Spares and Splits

Don't fret if you have not yet become particularly accomplished at covering spares and your practice habits regarding this aspect of bowling are less than stellar. At least you can take solace in knowing that you have lots of company. I can't think of any aspect of our sport in which so many participants so needlessly fall short so often.

While the strength in numbers is comforting, there's no reason why you can't consistently fill frames. Paying attention to these skills will pay great dividends. As with most bowlers, the primary culprits that you must overcome are ignorance of proper technique and strategy, married to neglect.

Bowlers generally don't practice enough. And the ones who do practice tend to forget that there's more to the sport than merely attempting to accumulate as many strikes as possible.

I've always found it amazing how many otherwise accomplished players who ought to know better exhibit indifference—or, worse yet, outright belligerence—toward spare shooting. After the introduction of urethane balls in the early 1980s sent scores soaring, the standing joke on the PBA Tour was that shooting spares was only for women and children. (Please don't take offense; I'm merely the messenger, and the views of some of my less politically correct colleagues don't necessarily reflect my own.)

Such is the stigma attached to anyone who has the audacity to take pride in his spare shooting that one would almost think that this is an item that ought not to be discussed in mixed company. It's kind of like that idiosyncratic spinster aunt; it's fine to visit her for the holidays but, for heaven's sake, don't be seen together in public!

While covering a spare might not have the macho appeal of scattering and shattering a full rack of pins, it's an aspect of the game that you neglect at your peril. Every frame that you fail to fill requires a double as compensation. The traditional adage is to first learn to make spares and the strikes will come.

Just by staying "clean" (avoiding any open frames), you can shoot as much as 190 even without rolling a single strike. A clean game with an occasional strike but without a double will usually put you well into the 190s, assuming that you obtain decent count in most of your frames. A clean game with a double will generally put you on the happy side of 200. Make it a turkey instead of a double and you'll probably be in the two-teens. And so on right on up the line.

All of which means that, as with golf, you can shoot some pretty decent scores merely by avoiding trouble. If you can simply improve to where you

An avid golfer (and all-out competitor in any sport that he plays), the incomparable Earl Anthony appreciates the importance of covering his spares so as not to beat himself. *Courtesy of the PBA*

make one more spare per game, you will add 10 pins to your average. Make four more spares on a night of league play and you'll make the jump from averaging 148 to 161.

If you're not yet sold on the merits of this chapter, here's an odd "coincidence" to consider: The list of bowling's all-time greatest players and its finest spare shooters is virtually identical. Compared to Dick Weber covering a single-pin leave, the sun rising in the east is a hit-ormiss proposition. Mark Roth and Earl Anthony weren't far off Mr. Weber's standards. Of today's superstars, no one is more consistently accurate than Walter Ray Williams.

Do you notice a pattern developing here?

So do I. Which is why I have always taken my spare and split shooting seriously. I view them as a great opportunity to make up ground on players who have more power than I and can outstrike me, but whose carelessness on second shots tosses away valuable wood.

In every PBA tournament I have entered, I have kept track of the number of splits I converted as well as the amount of spares that I missed. At the end of the week I compare those two figures. I'm content when the number of splits that I made exceeds the number of spares that I'd blown. Conversely, I'm never pleased with myself when those stats were the wrong way around.

To me, those numbers are the equivalent of a football team's turnovers versus the opposition miscues they recover. In virtually every case, a team that is well into the plus category will contend for a championship. Teams in turnover arrears tend to hold up the standings.

As far as I'm concerned, any week in which I am on the plus side constitutes a successful tournament. I feel as if I have recovered more fumbles than I've thrown interceptions.

And, like avoiding a football turnover, your ability not to beat yourself with silly open frames will give you more confidence. It also provides a psychological edge in match play. Your opponent knows that he will have to bowl well to beat you and will have to string strikes in order to come from behind.

In one way, my less-educated peers are right. Spares are for women and children. But they're also for boys and men.

MISTAKE 62

Too Much Power to the People

There are two varieties of spares; those that involve double wood (any combination of the 1-5, 2-8, and/or 3-9) and those that don't. Into the latter category add the 1-3-6-9 and the 1-2-4-8.

For non–double-wood spares, you do not need to hook the ball. Covering a lot of boards gains power, but power isn't needed in this situation. Thus, to throw a big hook at a non–double-wood spare is silly as it sacrifices accuracy, which is the one ingredient that does matter. All you need to do is put the ball in the right spot and the spare will be made.

If you tend to hook the ball a lot, you should discover how to throw it straight. Few pros have ever put more into their strike ball than Bob Learn, Jr. He employs a cupped wrist that's combined with extraordinary lift and turn. As Bob releases the ball he raises upward with his body in an effort to put every ounce of his power into every strike shot. Although his style is somewhat unorthodox, it definitely works for him. Such is Bob's power that he ranks among the sport's all-time leaders for sanctioned perfect games.

On April 8, 1996, he put on one of the most remarkable performances in the sport's history. Rolling in front of a near-capacity crowd of hometown supporters in the Erie (Pennsylvania) Civic Center and a national television audience, Bob captured the Flagship Open by defeating Johnny Petraglia, John Mazza, Parker Bohn III, and Randy Pedersen. His scores of 300, 270, 280, and 279 provided a 1129 total that shattered David Ozio's old record of 1070. Bob's 850 for the first three games easily erased Jim Stefanich's 21-year-old standard of 815.

Yes, Bob Learn, Jr., can throw strikes with the best of them. But it wasn't until he greatly improved his spare shooting that he became a bona fide force on the PBA Tour. To do that he had to learn how to throw the ball straight. For his non–double-wood spares, Bob now bends his wrist backward, lengthens his backswing to generate additional ball speed, keeps his hand behind the ball throughout his swing rather than rotating it during his release, and doesn't hit upward on his follow-through. On top of that, he uses a hard-shell ball that's designed to hook very little.

Even someone who generates incredible carrying power on his strike ball like Bob Learn, Jr., must still be able to fill frames. *Courtesy of the PBA*

We can all learn from Learn. My advice: For all non–double-wood spares, throw your ball straight by emulating his formula. Think of the delivery as if you were pitching a softball.

The only controversial item on Learn's agenda involves using a different ball for most of his spare and split shots than the one that he uses to throw strikes. The advantage is that a ball that's designed to skid on a lane will cover fewer boards. This is a great edge, especially in cases in which lanes aren't oiled evenly from gutter to gutter.

A porous (soft-shell) strike ball that encounters an unexpectedly dry area on the lane will break too much, which will cause it to almost certainly hook past the pin(s). This is a key consideration on cross-lane shots given that your ball will be crossing boards that aren't being frequently used. Predicting the amount of oil on them isn't easy.

There are, however, two disadvantages to changing equipment. One issue involves cost and convenience. Purchasing a second ball plus a double-ball bag at today's prices isn't an inexpensive investment. It also means that you will have to lug more than 30 pounds of equipment to and from the center. That's no minor matter if, like me, you live in a climate where you have to transport yourself over snow- and ice-covered parking lots. Nor is it exactly easy on the body, particularly if you, like me, have a birth certificate that's gotten a bit yellow around the edges!

By far the more significant consideration is that no two bowling balls can be drilled exactly alike. Even though an experienced pro shop operator will attempt to duplicate the feel of your strike ball, they won't be identical. Any difference could become greater as one ball is used more frequently than the other or if you put more tape in one ball's thumb hole.

I speak from some painful personal experience. In the semifinal match of the 1982 Toledo Trust PBA National Championship, I faced Charlie Tapp for the right to meet Earl Anthony in the title game. Charlie beat me because I missed a 10 pin. I switched to a harder ball, but it slipped off my hand and disappeared into the gutter. Disappearing with it was at least $9,000 (the difference between $20,000 for being runner-up versus $11,000 for third) and, perhaps, $27,000 (had I won that game and gone on to defeat Earl, I would have earned $38,000). Throw in a few extra grand in manufacturer's incentives and endorsements and I'm sure you can understand why I'd like to be able to have that shot back.

It was just one of those things; the ball slipped off my thumb. With hindsight, I realize that I probably should have blown into the thumb hole to

As far as I'm concerned, Charlie Tapp had enough talent that I shouldn't have treated him so generously! *Courtesy of the* PBA

create a little moisture so as to help me hang on to the ball better.

If you're a player who has problems cutting down on your hook through physical changes, then you will have no choice but to switch balls. If you can throw even a soft-shell ball fairly straight, the change might not be justified.

However, one equipment adjustment is always appropriate. Players who wear a wrist device that's designed to increase hook should remove it for all non–double-wood spare and split attempts.

MISTAKE 63

Not Realizing That Light Makes Might

The more ball speed you generate, the less your ball should hook. How-ever, you don't want to heave the ball, because doing so requires such a muscled swing that it's easy for your armswing's alignment to go awry.

Aside from holding the ball higher during your address to add to the height of the backswing, you can also use a lighter ball. This is something that I heartily recommend to players who are either fairly light or who are only young at heart. Far too many senior men stubbornly stick with a 16-pound ball. There's just no reason for that, especially on spares in which power is irrelevant. Go as light as a 12-pound ball so that it will be easy to generate greater speed.

MISTAKE 64

Going up the Boards

The first elementary rule is that for spares on the right you move your feet to the left on the approach. For spares on the left, you move to your right. For spares in the middle, you stay in the middle of the approach. This tac-tic gives your shot the best possible angle.

Shooting cross-lane at corner-pin leaves (defined here as the 7 or 10 pin) allows for a greater margin of error than if you threw the ball straight down

Regardless of which hand you use to throw the ball, move to the right to shoot a 7-pin spare (left) and to the left for a 10-pin spare (right).

the lane. Is it acceptable to stand all the way to the right to make a 10 pin? Yes, if you can make it consistently. What I'm offering aren't commandments. Instead, they are guidelines that should help you improve your conversion percentage.

MISTAKE 65

Not Knowing the Formulas

To again review a bowling lane's geography, each lane has 39 boards that run from the approach to the pindeck. Painted on every fifth board are arrows with corresponding dots at the foul line and on the approach at 12 and 15 feet from the line. The arrows are on the 5th, 10th, 15th, 20th (center), 25th, 30th, and 35th boards. Dots can be found on boards 10, 15, 20,

25, and 30, with some centers also including them on the 5th and 35th as well.

When I allude to your position on the approach, I'm referring to where you place the inside of your sliding foot (the left foot for a right-handed player or the right foot for a left-handed player). Thus, if I say to stand on the 20th board, you should place the inside of the sliding foot on the same board as the center dot is located.

At your next practice, begin by shooting the 3 pin (if you are left-handed start with the 2 pin). Stand around board 30 and aim for the third arrow. Assuming that you throw the ball in a manner that's fairly similar to your strike shot, this formula should work. This is generally the way to go if you roll your strike shots with either a modest amount of hook or fairly straight. These formulas don't apply if you have a big hook for strikes and subscribe to the modern theory of going straight at your spares.

Having said that, in a circumstance in which you have hit your target only to miss the pin, you should move your feet in the direction that you missed, keeping in mind that a move of one board on the approach equals a difference of one and a half boards in the opposite direction at the pins. Similarly, a half-board change of your feet translates to three-quarters of a board by the time your ball travels 60 feet.

Many pros do make half-board adjustments. However, for most amateurs the game never gets that precise. Use the 30th board-third arrow formula. This should work. But what to do if you make a quality shot and your ball rolls over the target only to miss the pin?

I suggest that you move two boards to compensate for the miss. Remember the rule that applies to both left- and right-handed players; if you miss to the right, move to the right. If you miss left, move left.

To the two-board change, add consideration for the margin by which you missed. If the ball barely failed to contact the pin, the initial two-board move ought to suffice. Should you have missed by one or two boards, move a total of three boards on the approach. If you missed by three to five boards, move a total of four boards with your feet.

The spot on the lane for the 3 pin (2 pin for lefties) will be the same as for the 9 pin (8 pin for lefties). Once you find a strategy for this shot you can adjust by moving three more boards to shoot a 6 pin and six boards for the 10 pin. In this case, a right-handed player will move to the left while a left-handed player moves to the right.

Taking that extra little bit of time to make certain that your feet are on the precise desired board is an essential element of consistently converting spares.

For the 9-10 split, a right-handed player stands a half-board to the right of where he or she normally stands to cover the 6 pin. To make the 7-8, a left-handed player moves a half-board to the left of her position used to cover a 4 pin.

Although the third arrow seems to be the most comfortable target for the majority of players, many pros prefer to move a bit farther with their feet in order to use the center arrow. That's because there is likely to be a greater accumulation of lane dressing in the center. Rolling through that will keep the ball going straight for a longer period of time.

MISTAKE 66

Not Having a Back-Up Plan

Many right-handed bowlers experience the most trouble with the 10 pin, while left-handers struggle with the 7 pin. More often than not, the biggest problem involves a lack of confidence. That channel is looming, and the fear of your ball disappearing into bowling's equivalent of quicksand conspires against your making a good shot.

If you fall into this category, here's an alternative approach to using the third or the fourth arrow as your target. Let's say that for your strike deliveries the inside edge of your left foot is on the 18th board (which is between the third and the center arrow) and you're using the second arrow for your strike line. In most cases in which you've left the corner pin, you have just hit the pocket. Make a simple adjustment. Move your feet 10 boards to the left for a 10 pin or 10 boards to the right for a 7 pin while maintaining the same target. Now pretend that you're throwing your strike ball.

This should allow you to enjoy success if you make a quality shot. The one disadvantage is that the angle is not quite as great as with the aforementioned strategy. As such, it will be a bit tricky for the bowler with a pronounced hook, and you'll have slightly less margin for error because there's less of an angle.

MISTAKE 67

Forgetting to Bring Your Key

In any multiple-pin spare there is a *key pin*. It is the pin with which your ball must make contact if you're to convert the spare. It's always the lowest-number pin since that's the one closest to you.

Thus, for the 2-5 you aim for the 2 pin. For the 3-6 you need to make contact with the 3 pin. Because multiple-pin leaves require the ball to also make contact with a second pin, you will want your ball not to hit the center of the key pin. A very slight adjustment of where you stand on the approach will accomplish this objective.

Making contact with the key pin is required to convert multiple-pin leaves such as the 2-4-5 (left), 3-6-10 (center), or 1-2-4 (right).

Not Knowing How to Shoot off the Strike Line

The spares that should be converted most often are the ones in which you can use the same target on the strike line while adjusting your position on the approach. What I'm about to offer are the formulas that have worked for me during my career, so perhaps a disclaimer is in order. These moves will work if you throw a fairly straight ball on your conversion attempt and if the lane oil is relatively even from gutter to gutter. But an equal application of dressing usually only exists just after the lanes have been serviced. Most centers will have more oil in the center of the lanes than on the outside. You will probably have to move a board or two to climb over that mountain of oil that's in the middle of the lane.

Because of these considerations, there are no rules that are set in stone. You may have to move your feet more or less than I'm recommending. Discovering the formula that works best for your game involves trial and error.

For a 2 pin, move four boards to the right on the approach while maintaining the same target as on your strike shot. To cover the 3 pin, move four boards to your left. The 4 pin calls for an eight-board move to your right. Move eight boards to your left for the 6 pin. The 8 pin calls for a five-board move to your right; the 9 pin calls for a five-board move to your left. The 5 pin is shot using one's strike line. However, if a lot of your hits have been light, you may want to move one board in the direction of your bowling hand (right-handers to the right and left-handers to the left). If you're inclined to shoot the corner pins (the 7 pin and the 10 pin) off your strike line, you will need to move 12 boards.

For the 2-4-5, move four boards to the right. For the 3-5-6, move four boards to the left. However, if the bucket (3-5-6-9 or 2-4-5-8) is standing that now becomes a double-wood spare. Your ball will have to drive through the front pin and not deflect too much or the back pin will remain. A five-board move is my preference. Be aware that the danger is the possibility of hitting that front pin flush so as to chop the 5 pin. That's why an alternative strategy that's used by several pros is to go hard and straight right up the boards.

The traditional baby split for a righty is the 3-10 (the 2-7 for a lefty). For this conversion or for the 3-6-10 (right) and the 2-4-7 (lefty), I move five boards away from my bowling hand and attempt to throw my normal strike shot. This should still work for you even if you hook the ball a lot. The only variable involves an overreaction when your ball hits the dry part of that lane.

I stand two boards to the left of my strike line to convert the 5-7 (while a left-hander should stand five boards to the left). For the 5-10 the move is to your right; five boards if you're a right-handed player and two boards if you're left-handed.

On occasion I've missed the 5-7 (5-10 for a lefty) due to an overreaction of the lane. That has seemed to happen more and more frequently of late with my ball getting too much of the 5 pin. If that's true for you, try moving two and a half or three boards.

The tape indicates where I was placing the inside of my sliding (left) foot for my strike shots. Notice how I have moved my feet two boards left to convert the 5-7 split (a left-handed player moves three boards to the right for the 5-10).

There are two schools of thought for the 4-7-10, 4-10, and 4-9 (for right-handers) and for the 6-7-10, 6-7, and 6-8 (for left-handers). You can opt to move 17 boards in the direction of your bowling hand while maintaining that strike line. Most pros prefer to change balls and attempt to hit the corner pin flush. That should send the 4 pin (righty) or the 6 pin (lefty) sliding across the lane toward the far-sided corner pin.

Please be aware that not everyone subscribes to my formulas. Most beginner classes recommend moves of three, six, and nine boards. As I have said before, a bit of experimentation on your part will uncover the strategy that works best for you.

Some splits can be shot off one's strike line. The washout, while technically not officially counted as a split, requires you to clip the side of the headpin and send it into a corner pin. Usually, a right-hander faces the 1-2-4-10 or 1-

Clip the far side of the headpin to cover the washout.

2-4-7-10, while a left-hander is confronted with the 1-3-6-7 or the 1-3-6-7-10.

With all of these combinations, your objective is to cross over the headpin to produce a Brooklyn hit. Move five boards in the direction of your bowling hand and attempt to throw the ball in the exact same manner—and with the identical target—as your strike shots.

In most cases, the baby split is found on the same side of the lane as the bowling hand. Thus, right-handers often face the 3-10 while southpaws see the 2-7. However, when this situation is reversed, I attempt to place my ball so it hits the far (left) side of the 2 pin with my ball, deflecting it into the 7 pin. This can be accomplished by moving 12 boards in the direction of your bowling hand.

MISTAKE 69

Seeing Double

The two double-wood combinations that occur with any prevalence are the 2-8 and the 3-9. These, too, can most simply be dealt with by using your strike line and strike delivery coupled with moving your feet. For the 2-8, I move five boards to my right (a lefty moves five left for the 3-9). For the 3-9, I move four boards to my left. If you're left-handed, move four boards to your right to cover the 2-8. While it's rare that you'll face the 1-5, the solution is to throw your strike ball.

Summary

Bowlers, as a whole, are very generous people. While donating to charity is admirable, there's nothing noble about donating pins. You should make filling frames as much of a priority as honing your strike shot delivery. To that end, always keep in mind the following factors:

1. To obtain the optimum angle, shoot spares and splits cross-lane by standing to the left of the approach for right-sided leaves, and to the right for left-sided conversion.
2. On non–double-wood covers, use the hard and straight strategy and a hard-shell ball.
3. For each specific spare and split, know the formulas to move the appropriate number of boards on the approach.
4. Alternatively, be able to make the proper adjustments to shoot spares and splits off of your strike line.

CHAPTER 9

Practice

An Achilles' heel that afflicts the great majority of today's bowlers is bad practice habits. As a group, we don't practice nearly enough and, when we do, it tends not to be sufficiently well structured to give the maximum benefit. As a result, not enough of us fulfill our potential.

In this chapter I will offer a few ideas on how you can work on your own (or with a personal coach) to improve your game. Of course, I'm of the belief that watching those bowling tips on ESPN telecasts featuring Mr. Average Builder (i.e., me) wouldn't hurt!

It's very important that you define the area of your game that's most in need of attention and then work hard on it. I'm sure that every successful professional bowler would concur with my sentiment that there's no substitute for good practice habits.

MISTAKE 70

Failing to Work on Improving Your Game

In my opinion, there's nothing wrong with not practicing if you view bowling merely as a form of recreation with a bit of exercise thrown in for good measure. To those who simply enjoy the sport as a night out with friends, I say that's great as long as your pleasure isn't compromised when your score fails to meet your expectations. If that's the case, there's little reason for you to spend the time and money to practice.

If the number of pins you knock over does matter to you, then it's important that you practice with a purpose. To really become good requires that you work regularly or, if possible, on a daily basis. At the very least, the amount of time you spend practicing should be equal to the total time you spend competing.

I never could figure out why so many fairly good bowlers lack the discipline to practice as much as do our counterparts in other sports. For example, there's an entire industry of training facilities for golf. Ever see the bowling equivalent of a driving range? Me neither. There's a good reason for that; just how long do you think such a place would stay in business if it catered only to the practice needs of bowlers?

Moreover, very few amateurs seek out a local pro from whom they can take lessons. Even fewer have a well-conceived and well-executed practice regimen.

Instead, most bowlers only "improve" after buying a new piece of equipment. Even after spending hundreds of dollars on shoes, balls, and assorted paraphernalia, they seem to remain content to make the same mistakes week after week. I find their attitude baffling.

Personally, I will never be satisfied or complacent with my game. As far as I'm concerned, there are only two types of athletes: those who work hard to improve and the remainder. If you're in the latter category, you're actually getting worse compared to your more ambitious opponents.

The requirements to become a top-class player in any sport include a willingness to practice religiously. To me, an empty center represents an opportunity to fulfill my dreams.

MISTAKE 71

Employing Your Math Skills

When you're competing, the objective of bowling is simple: Produce a higher score than your opponent. To help me do that, I don't keep score when I'm practicing. This philosophy is grounded in my desire to avoid the emotions I feel when I either exceed or fail to meet my expectations. My purpose during practice sessions isn't to compete, but to improve. Becoming distracted by my score would be counterproductive to meeting my objective.

If you must keep track with a pencil and paper, here's an alternative. For every strike, give yourself one point. Should all of the pins end up in the pit, you get an extra point. Subtract one point for every nonstrike. Your challenge is to stay above par.

MISTAKE 72

To Practice Long Is to Practice Wrong

There's no inherent correlation between the amount of time allocated to practice and the benefits that you reap. Some players, like PBA star David Ozio, regularly engage in marathon sessions. That's fine for David because he has the discipline to fully focus for several hours at a time. As such, his work bears fruit.

However, most of us have less generous attention spans. As soon as I find that my concentration has wandered, I put my ball down and unlace my shoes. To continue to bowl at that point wouldn't be worthwhile. In fact, it would probably become counterproductive. To roll poor shot after poor shot would harm my confidence as well as hinder my physical skills.

So, too, I stop when the aches and pains associated with overusing muscles become a factor. If, for example, your back is so sore that you can't bend properly at the foul line during your release, it is likely that you'll compensate by staying more upright. To practice in this manner isn't conducive to improving your delivery. It's almost certain to lead to bad habits.

Speaking of discomfort, you must cope with some minor irritants when competing. All of us have had to deal with the loss of skin on our bowling hands. When that occurs in practice, I patch up just like I would in competition. I stop my session only when the amount of discomfort is so significant that it causes me to deliver shots in an awkward manner.

MISTAKE 73

Failing to Plan

Far too many bowlers put about as much thought into mapping out their practices as a squirrel puts into crossing the street. The result of such short-sightedness is as predictable as it is regrettable and avoidable.

To avert being squashed by the tires of tenpin mediocrity, always arrive at the lanes with something specific on which to work. For example, let's say that you have noticed that your shots aren't as accurate as you would like. You have further diagnosed the causes as inconsistent timing coupled with a bad armswing.

Either by having someone who knows your game observe you in action, by consulting videotape, or by self-diagnosis, you further decide that both problems are rooted in your pushaway. On some shots you hand the ball out in a direction away from your body. Sometimes you begin your push-away too late and, on other occasions, too early. To make matters worse, the length varies. As a result, your feet are rarely in sync with your arm-swing at the point of release.

So today you will concentrate on your pushaway. Your next session might focus on bending the bowling knee on your next-to-last step, your balance at the finish position, converting cross-lane spares, or attempting different angles to the pocket with your strike shots. Or it could be any of countless other items.

No matter what the topic, it's vitally important to have something specific to work on. I never work on two things at once. Doing so virtually assures that you won't do either one justice. That's because bowling is a game of concentration in which you must learn to shut out distractions. The ability to focus on what you want to do at that given time is key. If you're working on one thing, you have to give it your full attention at that time. My personal formula is simple: To accomplish a lot, I concentrate on a little. To assure that I accomplish very little, I would merely have to try to concentrate on a lot of things.

MISTAKE 74

Exceeding the Speed Limit

It's important that you don't just throw balls. An honest effort is required with each delivery if you're to get better.

I find that I must regulate the pace at which I bowl. In a game, several natural breaks occur when it's someone else's turn to shoot. The natural tendency in practice to rush shot after shot should be resisted. I find that the rhythm that occurs in competition is more conducive to achieving consistency.

That doesn't mean that I wait four minutes between frames as I might when rolling on a five-player team. But it does mean that I make a conscious effort to pause for at least 30 seconds after every other frame (since we pros roll two frames at a time).

Maintaining a match-realistic rhythm is what works best for me. However, through trial and error you may discover that your needs are different. Go with what best suits your needs.

MISTAKE 75

Going Kaput by Staying Put

When working on producing strikes, I either shadow bowl or I ignore whatever pins remain standing on the second shot so as to roll another strike shot.

I recommend practicing from different angles. It's human nature to get score-conscious, pocket-conscious, and ego-conscious. Always remember that the only score that matters is what you roll in competition, not what you produce in practice.

One training game I play is to roll five consecutive shots on a normal strike line. For the sixth through tenth shots I move five boards to the left with my feet while also moving my target three boards in the same direction (left-handed players move their feet and target to the right). I make another 5-3 move for the following five shots. When I get all the way to the left side of the approach, I then work my way back across the lane by moving 5-3 to my right.

This formula should work unless the lanes are blocked. The 5-3 moves may also force you to slightly adjust your speed. As noted previously, more speed is usually required when playing up the boards, while a slower shot tends to work better when using a deep inside line.

Every so often I'll make a 10-6 move or, if I feel really daring, a 15-9 adjustment. And I'll do it using the exact same speed.

You can practice by playing one lane from one angle and the other lane on that pair from a different angle. The first time I appeared on a television show on Tour was in Edison, NJ. I faced Nelson Burton, Jr., who was playing the gutter on one lane and fourth arrow on the other. He began with six in a row at me. It was certainly a baptism by fire, underscoring to me the importance of working in practice to become a more versatile player.

Toward that end, you can try one release on one lane and a different one on the other. Or you can fiddle around with different speeds. As per Earl Anthony's example, practicing different speeds can help build a calculator in your head so you can throw the same way every time at whatever speed you're trying to achieve.

The way I've scored in some tournaments might have suggested I was bowling with my eyes closed, but that's something I do only in practice!

Practice in a way that is match-realistic. Shoot one frame on the left lane and the next on the right. By having to change angles, speeds, and releases with each shot, you will challenge yourself to be a better player. Gaining the confidence to do this in practice will allow you to try it in competition. This will give you a great edge when you're faced with a pair in which the oil patterns are dissimilar.

The changing of strike lines after each shot is a challenge, to say the least. When playing a line that's not one's natural angle, there's a tendency to try to clean up the shot by steering the ball at the target. Learning to be confident enough to let the ball do the work isn't an easy matter. Always remember that old bowling mantra: Trust is a must or your game is a bust.

However, if you just can't avoid steering your shots, here's an exercise to try. Close your eyes during your next-to-last step (just before you begin your slide). Doing so puts the target in your mind's eye, removes all fear from your delivery, and eases your follow-through.

MISTAKE 76

Not Challenging Yourself with Inferior Equipment

If you're like me, when you fork over $140 to a pro shop proprietor, you want a bowling ball that could knock over the World Trade Center. So why use a ball that hits like a featherweight and couldn't carry a half-hit if your life depended on it?

The answer is that using the "wrong" ball in practice will force you to execute perfectly in order to strike. So on an oily lane, I might just use a harder-shell ball. Or on a dry lane, I'll try a porous-surface ball because it will make being accurate a greater challenge. The use of counterproductive equipment has helped me to become a better shot-maker.

MISTAKE 77

Forgetting Huey Lewis's Advice

The rocker Huey Lewis sang some great advice for us bowlers—it's hip to be square. That's especially true for the occasional participant who finds repeating motions difficult enough without introducing superfluous movements into her delivery.

Here's a practice pointer to help in that regard. Just after executing your pushaway, put your nonbowling arm out. Point it toward the opposite wall of the center. This will square your shoulders so that you're not leading with your nonbowling shoulder. This is especially important if you're going up the boards.

The ability to loft shots to get your ball through the head area of the lane can be honed by rolling over a towel.

MISTAKE 78

Not Learning How to Alter
Your Landing Zone

Great players have an arsenal of adjustments at their disposal, including the ability to loft a shot beyond a very dry head area or laying the ball short when needed.

Lofting a ball isn't to be confused with tossing it upward. You must still execute a good release and be well balanced at the line. To practice getting the ball farther down the lane on the fly, place a towel just beyond the foul line. Your shot must clear that towel on the fly *and* hit your target.

To lay a ball short, I simply concentrate on making certain that my thumb is removed from my ball by the bottom of my swing. I always naturally got my shots out onto the lane, so I found it difficult to lay the ball short (unless, of course, I was trying for a double, and then it was all too easy!).

MISTAKE 79

Not Hitting Your Stride

Chances are that you see yourself as a three-step, four-step, or five-step bowler. I like to practice all three options. There's nothing wrong with a five-step player practicing four steps if for no other reason than it makes you feel so good when you go back to your preferred method. Learning to coordinate your armswing with different numbers of steps helps to develop a better feel for proper timing. I've found that this has helped me to make a subconscious adjustment during my delivery on occasions when my timing was out of sync toward the start of my delivery.

MISTAKE 80

Only Competing in Competition

There's a big difference between throwing strike after strike in an empty center at 10 o'clock in the morning and doing the same in the tenth frame when a game is on the line. Like a gunfighter practicing against tin cans, your palms won't get sweaty until you're going up against an armed opponent.

But how does one replicate the pressure of a match in a practice environment? This is a key issue because the psychological parameters are of paramount importance in bowling. Like a field goal kicker or a soccer player taking a penalty kick, hundreds of pros can produce perfect form and results when there's no pressure involved. But the difference between the superstars and the also-rans owes as much (or more) to their ability to perform in the clutch. That's why the mental game is so vital to achieving success on the Pro Tour, where almost every player is gifted with outstanding physical skill.

Most pros roll practice matches against opponents of similar skill. To add pressure, I like to make a bet. Unlike some people who roll for large sums of money, my gambling takes the form of having the loser buy lunch. Even though the financial stakes aren't high, the pride factor of not wanting to be defeated with something on the line does add a certain degree of pressure. Learning to cope with a faster pulse rate before executing the game-deciding shot is important.

MISTAKE 81

Sparing the Details

I challenge anyone to name one truly great bowler who wasn't a first-rate spare shooter. Not beating yourself is every bit as important as throwing a powerful strike ball. The fact that the very best pros don't donate pins owes to their practice habits.

If you're economically minded, shoot your spare on the first ball of every frame. Save your strike shot for the second delivery.

Get your money's (and time's) worth out of practice by throwing your spare ball first.

Here's a great game to play to work on your cross-lane conversions. With a full rack, attempt to cleanly pick off the 10 pin on your first shot and the 7 pin on the next (vice versa for lefties).

This is one practice game in which you should keep score. The objective is to knock over as few pins as possible. Should your first shot fall into the channel, you're charged with a strike. Give yourself a spare should the second ball leave the lane. A perfect game is a 20.

MISTAKE 82

Lack of Vision

In an election year, we constantly hear public officials talking about their vision for America. Bowlers, too, need vision.

A few years ago the idea was put forward to place a large mirror a few feet above the lane at about the arrows. This device had enough room for the ball to roll beneath it. What made it a good teaching tool was that the player could see what he was doing. Although it never became very popular, it was like having your own built-in video camera.

Should you be unable to find a center that has such mirrors, take advantage of modern technology and have a friend or family member videotape your practice session. This can be a great diagnostic tool, and it can also help your self-esteem—I've found that a lot of times the bowler looks better than she thought she looked. In that regard, it can provide much-needed encouragement.

Changing the angle of the camera will allow you to analyze different aspects of your delivery. Shooting from behind will tell you if your pushaway and armswing are straight. Shooting from behind while prone (or crouched low) will provide a good study of your hand position throughout your delivery. Taping from the side will reveal whether your pushaway coincides with your first stride and whether your timing is consistent. Should the proprietor or manager allow the cameraperson to shoot from an adjacent lane, taping from in front will tell you a lot about your pushaway, armswing, and follow-through. It will also reveal whether your body remains square throughout the delivery and, more importantly, if it's square during your release.

The dropped shoulder.

I would encourage the person doing the taping to follow the ball down the lane so that you know the shot's result. This will prove quite helpful in solving a problem. For example, let's say that you have a tendency to miss your target to the right. By studying the shots in which your ball didn't get up to the pocket, you may notice a common flaw (such as dropping your right shoulder). This will tell you the key coaching point to remind yourself of while in competition.

When watching tapes of myself, the first thing that I look for is my timing. For me, it's important that the ball is at the peak of my backswing as my foot on my next-to-last

I don't even have to watch my ball to know where it's going; the follow-through tells all! Coming across my body (upper left) means I've attempted to steer my shot to the pocket, while having my hand fly away from my body (upper right) indicates that I tried to save a shot almost certainly destined to become a split. Every so often, I get it right (left)!

step hits the floor. When checking the side view, I always note the length of my pushaway and check to see if my foot and hand have moved simultaneously. I also notice whether that pushaway leads into a free armswing.

Like many players, on occasion I've been guilty of steering my shots at my target. The front angle will show me if my elbow has broken during my follow-through. If that's the case, I know that I attempted to guide the ball. This is a common flaw when under pressure, often caused by the fear of failure. Another cause could be something as simple as needing another piece of tape in my thumb hole.

A follow-through that goes to the inside is another sure sign of steering. This, too, will usually result in a light hit. Years ago, when equipment wasn't as advanced and the back end of the lane wasn't a player's best friend, an inside follow-through usually meant that the 4-5-7 would stare at you (or a 5-6-10 for a lefty). Although today's conditions are more forgiving, you still want to produce a good follow-through.

Summary

If results matter to you—I assume they must to some degree—you should put thought into designing your practice time. The hallmarks of a productive session are to identify an area of your game that's most in need of improvement, stick to one theme at a time, only work as long as you are able to fully concentrate, and perform at a match-realistic pace. Whenever possible, at least some of your practice time should include playing different parts of the lane, changing ball speed and releases, and practicing the covering of the various spare and split possibilities.

Finally, try to enlist the assistance of a qualified pro or a friend who knows your game, or take advantage of video equipment for self-analysis.

CHAPTER 10

The Mental Game

Aside from equipment considerations, all that we have touched upon so far has encompassed the physical actions that you must execute to make a good shot. While proper technique is a vital aspect of any sport, it's only a part of the overall equation.

Just as important as acquiring the skill to make good shots is having the proper temperament. An exceptional physical game without a strong mental game (or vice versa) isn't a whole lot more useful than owning a buggy without having a horse to pull it.

The two important aspects of your thought process are your attitude toward bowling and your attitude toward competing. The former involves taking the sport seriously. The latter involves not taking it so seriously that you place undue pressure on yourself to perform.

The biggest battle that I have fought throughout my entire career wasn't with an opponent. It wasn't with the pins. Nor was it with the lane conditions. My biggest battle has always been with myself to truly believe in myself.

From the time that our moms read to us from *The Little Engine That Could*, we all realized that a positive outlook enables us to accomplish more. However, knowing the value of being confident and really being confident are two very different things. That's especially true on those days when you're struggling.

Later in this chapter I will address the issues related to maintaining a positive approach. But, first, let's talk a bit about your attitude toward bowling.

The vast majority of the tens of millions of Americans who hit the lanes every year view bowling as a form of recreation. Only to a small percentage of us is it a highly competitive endeavor. For those who compete on the PBA and LPBT circuits, or in top-level amateur events, bowling is a sport. As such, I try to give myself any legal advantage that I can. That's why I make it a point to try to always eat right, get adequate sleep, and stay in shape.

But even if I were a once-a-week bowler who rolled in a mixed league, my pride would insist that I make an effort to do my best. A lesson from my parents that has long stuck with me is that anything that's worth doing is worth doing to the best of one's ability.

Does that mean that you must so concentrate on your game that you can't be sociable between shots? Of course not. Even on the men's and women's Pro Tours, scores of players chat with their fellow bowlers, friends, and fans during a block. Many of bowling's top stars are convinced that doing so helps them to stay relaxed.

What is essential is that you give yourself the opportunity to do your best. That should begin even before you arrive at the lanes.

MISTAKE 83

Not Taking Care of Business

If you're like most of us, the monetary value of your bowling equipment is not an inconsiderable total. Treat it accordingly. Contrary to some people's sentiments, bowling shoes are not allergic to shoe polish! Although you might not know it from observing some people's bowling towels, it is permissible to drop them into the washing machine every once in a while. Nor will it do you any great harm to transport your bag from the car to a place in the home where it won't be subjected to extreme heat or cold.

Many bowlers treat the trunk of their car like it's a storage area. Letting your ball bounce around back there isn't a particularly good idea for either the ball or your vehicle. Moreover, in the cold of winter and the heat of summer, the temperature inside the trunk can be as cold as a freezer or as hot as a furnace. That, in turn, makes the surface of your ball either harder (in winter) or softer (in summer). This will cause it to either not grip the lane (cold) or overreact (hot). Moreover, the ball's characteristics will slowly be altered during your league play as it moves toward room temperature.

MISTAKE 84

Neglecting to Check Equipment Prior to Usage

I recommend that you go through a checklist to make certain that your shoes and bowling balls are ship-shape before they're put to use. Observe the bottoms of your shoes to ensure that no foreign substance is present. Make it a point to check whether either shoelace has become frayed. Should that be the case, replace it before bowling (once you begin competing, you don't want to have to waste time between frames by digging through a side panel of your bag to find the extra set of laces).

Because the size of your thumb varies, always test each ball to see if it fits properly. Quite often, you will find it necessary to either insert or remove tape from the thumb hole. I also suggest that you wipe each ball with your bowling towel to remove any dust, dirt, oil, or resin.

MISTAKE 85

Failing to Prepare the Body for Physical Activity

Let's be honest—bowling three games isn't as demanding on the body as running a marathon or playing basketball. Nevertheless, bowling is a physical activity, and you should treat it accordingly.

All pros arrive at the lanes long before they're scheduled to begin competing. We engage in a comprehensive stretching regimen that includes our wrists, shoulders, hamstrings, quadriceps, and groin. I roll my first few practice shots gently. I walk slowly to the line, use a much shorter armswing, and drop the ball onto the lane. It takes me three or four deliveries in which

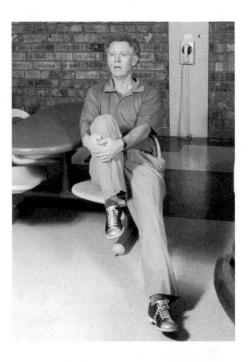

A comprehensive stretching routine is even more essential for older players.

I progressively throw the ball with more impetus until my body is prepared to execute an all-out attempt. The failure to take a lot off your first few warm-up rolls could result in an injury.

Most bowling centers allot five minutes for warm-up prior to league play. That should provide enough time for you to roll at least the equivalent of three or four frames. Once I'm loose, I make the most of that time by attempting a cross-lane spare on my first ball and then a strike shot on the subsequent delivery. The time to discover that the oil is uneven in the center of the lane is when shooting a 7 or a 10 pin before it counts on the scoresheet.

All of this boils down to paying attention to detail. Unfortunately, the only detail to which most bowlers pay any attention is to complain at great length to management about the state of the lanes!

MISTAKE 86

Forgetting to Have a Plan of Attack

Because my warm-up period is limited, I don't have adequate time to experiment with a wide variety of balls, angles, speeds, and releases. Instead, I must make an educated guess as to what combination of the above will provide me with the greatest margin for error.

Chances are, you have a preferred strike line and a favorite ball. Once your body is prepared for activity, it is essential that you properly execute your strike shots during practice. Only by doing so will you be able to read the result. Did your ball drift a few boards high? If so, try the adjustment that you guess is appropriate.

What should you do after executing a strong release and hitting the pocket, only to have your shot be DOA (dead on arrival) as it arrives at the pocket? The answer could lie in changing balls or to play a different part of the lane.

In a professional tournament, where one errant shot can mean thousands of dollars, I don't want to waste a lot of frames with trial and error. That's why I do a lot of scouting prior to bowling. Attend any pro tournament, and you will find the center packed during the final few games of a block. The players who will bowl next are observing how the lanes are reacting.

I attempt to discover two very important items. First, how are the players who are scoring the best playing the lanes? I look at their strike line, the equipment they're using, even whether their wrists are cupped.

The second half of the equation is to watch players whose styles are similar to mine. That will tell me what is likely to work for me and what strategies to avoid.

Very few amateurs are as attuned to the sport. Nor should they be. Nevertheless, you should have an idea of what you want to try. And you should make an effort to warm up properly so that you can determine whether your strategy is likely to work or if adjustments are in order.

MISTAKE 87

Not Being a Boy Scout

Bowlers should heed the Boy Scout motto of always being prepared. Instead, many of them are in the lounge, the bathroom, or at the snack bar when it's their turn to bowl. If you must visit one of those locales, have the consideration to inform your fellow players. Doing so will allow them to bowl around you until you return.

Too often, the AWOL competitor holds up the game and then reappears at a full sprint. That player then neglects the pre-shot routine, including the very important consideration of checking their shoes to be certain no foreign substance is present that could cause sticking or slipping at the line. At the very least, the lack of concentration on the task at hand will almost always guarantee a less than optimum delivery.

MISTAKE 88

Being a Soloist

Make no mistake about it, league bowling is a team sport. By cheering for each other and having a positive spirit you will gain both enjoyment and a competitive edge. The team that wins a championship isn't always the one

Providing help to teammates is an important ingredient in helping your team to succeed.

with the most talent. Quite often, it's the group of individuals who enjoy each other's company and help each other out.

When I bowl on a team, I make it my business to get to know the keys to success of my teammates. I can serve as a coach who notices when a player's timing is off, his armswing is out of alignment, or he's rearing up at the foul line. I always provide advice in a constructive manner.

When needed, provide empathy after an open frame. Picking up that teammate's psyche is important, which is why words of encouragement are always both appreciated and appropriate.

MISTAKE 89

Neglecting Common Courtesy

Before stepping onto the approach, make certain that bowlers aren't on either of the adjacent lanes. When two players arrive simultaneously, bowling etiquette calls for the person on the right to be granted the right-of-way. When you have concluded your delivery, watch the result, but then promptly return to the settee area so as not to delay the players on adjacent lanes.

You should enjoy your evening out, as long as your enthusiasm doesn't take away from other people's enjoyment. By all means, celebrate a great shot, but don't "run out" a strike by stepping onto a nearby lane or making such a commotion that other bowlers lose their concentration.

MISTAKE 90

Negative Self-Talk

As much as or more than any sport, bowling is a mental activity. The farther up the competitive ladder you can manage to climb, the more important your thought process becomes.

I must confess that I'm not an optimist by nature. As much as I have been able to accomplish during my career, I think I would have been far more successful had I been more positive. On almost any occasion when things didn't go my way, I would beat myself up. That occurred even though I fully appreciated the importance of maintaining a positive approach.

Even so, I'd tell myself things like "You stink," "You're a bum," "You're blowing it," "It's a good thing you're getting some bad breaks or you wouldn't get any breaks at all," and "What the heck are you doing out here?" My wife insists that she can walk into a center and immediately discern how I'm bowling by observing my body language. If my left hand is in my pocket or my shoulders are slumped, Debbie knows I'm struggling. For me not to yield to negative thoughts is a constant battle that I fight and only occasionally win.

In my defense, I must report that I have never beat myself up while performing on television. There is just too much at stake. I know that I can't expect to beat the best players in the world with the big money on the line unless I remain positive.

In contrast, Mike Aulby *always* looks as if things are going his way. Even when the pins aren't cooperating, he doesn't allow himself to get down. I only wish I had his personality. As good as his physical game is—and believe me, a guy who is a two-time Player of the Year must have a solid physical game—his mental approach is his greatest attribute by a wide margin. On a scale of 1 to 10, the mental games of Mike and Walter Ray Williams get a 10. At my best, I might have gotten up to a 6.

Fortunately, I am also extremely resilient. As much as I get on my own case, I can still focus on what I have to do in order to be successful on my subsequent shot.

One of the PBA's all-time greats was his own toughest critic. He

Mike Aulby's attitude gives him an enormous competitive edge. *Courtesy of the* PBA

would lose it whenever an opponent got a lucky break at a crucial point of a big match. In my opinion, his fiery temperament cost him hundreds of thousands of dollars and at least one dozen titles.

There is much to be said for keeping an even keel. One story that comes to mind involves game one of the 1969 World Series. The heavily favored Baltimore Orioles won that day over a New York Mets team that experts thought was overmatched.

As they walked toward the locker room, Mets team leaders Donn Clendenon and Tom Seaver were surprised to notice that the Orioles were engaged in a very spirited celebration. It then occurred to both of them that, just perhaps, the Orioles were that excited because they weren't fully certain that they'd win. The two Mets then relayed that message to their teammates, who proceeded to sweep the next four games!

Think about that for a minute. Here was an underdog team that had just lost the first game. But instead of being downcast, they found a positive note on which to build. That, in essence, underscores the importance of having a strong mental approach in sports.

Here's something to remember about self-talk. Always attempt to address yourself as if you were your own doubles partner.

MISTAKE 91

Refusing to Seek Help

No bowler's career better illustrates the vital nature of this aspect of our game than does that of John Mazza. Despite possessing obvious talent, his first few years on the PBA Tour can only be described as having been an unmitigated disaster. From 1982 through 1989, he entered 161 national tournaments without winning once. His total earnings were a paltry $129,345. He did improve in 1990, taking home $71,220 in 34 events, although he had yet to claim his first title.

John was beset with self-doubt. I suspect that he felt that he really wasn't good enough to challenge the big boys. No matter how many of his peers complimented him on his skills, John wasn't sold on John.

Unfortunately for him, perception is everything. It doesn't matter if everyone else thinks you are the greatest thing since the invention of the wheel.

It's how you see yourself that counts. If you see yourself as a failure, no amount of success will modify that sentiment.

Finally, John sought the aid of a sport psychologist. Their sessions focused entirely on dispelling his doubts. Once that was accomplished, John Mazza became a force with which the big boys had to reckon. From 1991 to 1995, he banked $427,650. During that period, he won six times in 115 tries. By having improved his mental game, he went from being an also-ran to a bona fide star.

At the PBA and LPBT levels, scores of players have the requisite physical ability to thrive. The difference between those who become stars and those who fall short can usually be found above the neck. Yes, some standouts, like me, beat themselves up with negative self-talk. I'm convinced that those individuals would have enjoyed far more success had they had a positive outlook like Walter Ray Williams or Mike Aulby.

One of the most remarkable displays I've ever witnessed of a strong mental game came during Walter Ray's march to his 20th career title during the 1996 Rochester (NY) Open. To join an elite fraternity whose membership, as of that time, was limited to Earl Anthony, Mark Roth, Don Johnson, Dick Weber, Mike Aulby, Marshall Holman, Pete Weber, and Dick Ritger required that Williams defeat three title-round foes.

That Walter Ray got the best of Norm Duke, Chris Hooper, and Pete Weber was no small feat since Duke and Weber rank among pro bowling's established veteran stars. What was truly impressive was that Walter had real difficulty carrying that night. Despite painting the pocket on virtually every shot, he averaged 232 during his three wins.

To be sure, 232 isn't a number to sneeze at. But it's hardly a great score when one is on target on shot

Positive self-talk has helped Walter Ray Williams to become the dominant player on the PBA Tour of the 1990s.
Courtesy of the PBA

after shot. Time after time he left solid 10 pins, including on his initial three deliveries of the title game. Suffering so much bad luck would have had a lesser man cursing the pin gods. But not Walter Ray.

Prior to that ESPN telecast he had agreed to wear a wireless microphone so that the rest of us could share his thoughts. Not once that night did I hear a negative utterance from his lips. Every comment—and I mean *every* comment—was positive and exhibited full confidence. I remember remarking on the air that it was one of the most incredible examples that I have ever encountered in the power of positive thinking.

MISTAKE 92

One Mistake per Customer

One of the best pieces of advice I ever received came from a youth basketball coach after I'd blown a lay-up. So angry was I with myself that I stood still while glaring at the rim. My coach told me that having missed the shot was a mistake, but so was my failure to run back on defense. He said that he could live with the first mistake since we all make physical errors. But he couldn't live with my mental miscue. "Don't make two mistakes" was his motto.

So, too, in bowling. We all make bad shots. A bad shot is a mistake. But becoming so angry that we lose our composure is to make the second mistake that my basketball coach warned against.

The primary theme that noted soccer coach Bora Milutinovic imparted to the U.S. National Team prior to the 1994 World Cup was that "the next play is the most important play." In bowling, your next shot is your most important shot. The reason: It's the only shot that you can affect.

That doesn't mean that any of us can apply 100 percent concentration to every delivery in every game. It's human nature to be more determined when you have a chance to produce a double, or a game's outcome is on the line entering the tenth frame. However, you should never dwell on your last shot. Once the ball has left your hand, there is absolutely nothing you can change. So don't make two mistakes. The top players rebound from an open frame by staying focused on the task at hand.

MISTAKE 93

Not Giving 100 Percent on Every Shot, Part I

What the 1984 PBA media guide called "the most bizarre finish in PBA tournament history" took place on June 11, 1983, at Gable House Bowl in Torrance, California. Top-seeded Don Genalo lost to Jimmie Pritts, Jr., 214–212. But it was how he lost that is forever etched into bowling folklore.

Thinking that he needed a mark to win, Genalo was distraught when he left the "Greek church split" (4-6-7-9-10) on the first ball of the tenth frame. Little did Don realize that merely covering the 6-9-10 would suffice to claim his third title in as many months. Instead, a disgusted Genalo tossed his last shot into the right channel.

Countless bowlers have reacted to a split just as Don did. But it was his blunder that became bowling's equivalent of Mickey Owen's passed ball or Jim Marshall running to the wrong end zone.

I always want to know the score, and, thus, what I need on my next shot; but I never allow myself to become preoccupied by the scoreboard or what's at stake. To bowl well, I must focus on my physical keys so as to make good shots.

The lesson that Don learned should be heeded by all of us who play sports. Always do your best on every shot. And, with a tip of the hat to Bora Milutinovic, remember that your next delivery is your most important shot.

MISTAKE 94

Not Giving 100 Percent on Every Shot, Part II

One of the most amazing experiences I ever encountered on the Tour happened when I was bowling with a young hotshot in the first round of a national event. He had a powerful hook ball that could slice through a mountain. Unfortunately, its power was exceeded by that of his temper.

During warm-ups it was clear that his strategy wasn't working. Nevertheless, he kept trying to overpower the lanes. When the bell rang, he hadn't even attempted a different approach. Predictably, he left difficult splits in each of his first two frames. His self-talk following the second delivery made it clear to me that he was already a beaten man.

Here it was but two frames into a 6-game block of the 18-game qualifying segment of a 42-game tournament. But his week was already over because he, in essence, quit on himself.

Let's give him the benefit of the doubt and assume that the lane conditions were so adverse to his game as to have made it impossible for him to have won that week. Even so, he should have had a back-up strategy that would have allowed him to compete for a berth in the match play portion of the event. Even if that fell short, he could have viewed the 18 qualifying games as a great practice opportunity to hone his skills under tournament lane conditions.

The peers that I respect the most *always* compete on every shot. Even when they're out of contention with five frames remaining, they are searching for a tactical solution so that they can be competitive the next time they bowl on a similar condition. That attitude is a big part of being a pro. It's also a big part of becoming the best player that your talent will allow.

MISTAKE 95

Being a Spectator

Shakespeare posed the question "To be or not to be?" The tenpin equivalent is "To watch or not to watch?"

There is no defense in bowling. Therefore, you gain little by watching your opponent bowl (the lone exception being if that person's game is so similar to your own that you can gain a strategic edge through observation).

A boyhood friend of mine introduced me to the concept of what he called "the demoralizer shot." That's the ball that lifts the spirits of one player while taking the wind out of the other bowler's sails. An example is carrying a lucky Brooklyn hit that's sandwiched between two strikes.

Those types of breaks will occur. Over the long haul, they tend to even out, so you shouldn't be concerned with whether you are receiving "justice" in a given game. Don't worry about what you can't control.

Don't look if an opponent's good luck tends to unnerve you.

The classic example of being totally focused on one's own game was provided by 1996 PBA Rookie of the Year C. K. Moore in his very first Tour event, the Columbia 300 Open at Austin, Texas's Highland Lanes.

After a shaky 173–166 win over Ed Richardson, C. K. showed a veteran's acumen by adjusting his strike line and changing to a ball that would hook less on the troublesome right lane. He beat Dave Traber to set up an apparent mismatch, pitting his $10,300 in career earnings in regional play against Parker Bohn III, an 11-time national champion with $1.1 million in official prize money.

C. K. told me that his strategy was "not to be overwhelmed because it is intimidating when you've got lights all over the place and it's that quiet. I can't affect my opponent's score, so there's no reason to worry about how he's bowling. As dumb as it sounds, I was just trying to bowl well."

While four of his first seven strikes were a bit questionable, there was nothing to question about Moore's final deliveries. He was so focused that he didn't even realize that he was working on a perfect game until thinking it odd that

C. K. Moore likes to joke that his initials stand for "Cosmo Kramer or Clark Kent, depending on how I'm bowling." To become a Superman on the lanes in Austin required a heightened mental state.
Courtesy of the PBA

Bohn raced onto the approach for the final frame. Parker's intent was to "get out of his way fast; it was his time for glory."

Only Bohn's rushing prompted Moore to glance at the scoreboard for the very first time. Unaware of the $25,100 perfect game bonus, he proceeded to roll three flush strikes.

Some pros talk of getting into a zone, but Moore was on another planet! All that he recalls is telling himself to make good shots, taking deep breaths, and receiving high-fives. Getting him to try to reconstruct his thought process during those three strikes is as futile as asking an Evander Holyfield knockout victim to describe what hit him.

MISTAKE 96

Not Knowing the Score

Being oblivious to the scoreboard worked well for C. K. Moore. Other players, however, want to know exactly what they need in any given situation. This is a particularly important aspect of match play.

Let's say that you're on a strike and up pops the 6-7-10 split. Do you go for it or settle for covering the 6-10? If you go for the conversion, you risk toppling only the 10 pin. Since you're on a strike, that would cost two pins off your score.

My decision would be predicated on a number of factors. If I'm behind and my opponent is bowling well, I would know that I couldn't afford an open frame. If I have a very emotional opponent and I'm brimming with confidence, I would go for it because of the opportunity to unnerve my rival.

However, let's say that covering the 6-10 would leave me up by 1, 11, or 21 pins but a miss would slice the margin to −1, 9, or 19 sticks. In that case I'd play it safe. If I maintain an 11-pin lead, my opponent would need a triple to go ahead, but he'd only need a double if I were up by 9.

It can be dangerous to be preoccupied with the scoreboard. Many players become tense when they focus on what they need rather than concentrating on how to execute a good shot. Another hazard is to become conservative. Needing but a mark to win, some players will throw a defensive shot so as to avert a split. The axiom on the pro tours is that the best mark is a strike.

The key is to know yourself. If you thrive on pressure, you may want to know what you need in the tenth frame. Conversely, if you will become distracted by such considerations, ignore the scoresheet and just think about your mechanics and strategy.

MISTAKE 97

Think Long, Think Wrong

The time for analysis is when you're on the bench. That's when I concentrate on possible adjustments and what I must do on my subsequent shot. However, once I step onto the approach, the time for thinking is over. I engage in my pre-shot routine and only ponder the most important physical key that I must execute properly while concentrating on my target.

MISTAKE 98

Not Exploiting the Power of Your Imagination

When I learned to bowl, all of the instructional material dealt with throwing the ball properly. Coaching has evolved since then. Today's Team USA members are taught how to exploit mental imaging to their advantage.

That technique involves shutting your eyes, closing out all distractions, and picturing yourself executing the perfect delivery. Envision your ball rolling over your target and driving through the pocket to shatter the rack. Having done that, remind yourself of the many times in the past that you did exactly what you wanted to do with a shot. Tell yourself, "I did it then and I'm going to do it again now."

MISTAKE 99

Being as Tight as the Proverbial Drum

Ask a pro who choked on a pressure shot what went wrong and, if she is honest, you'll usually hear a confession such as, "I squeezed it."

It's not unusual to grip the ball more tightly on an important delivery. But doing so makes it far more difficult to produce a clean release and an armswing that's controlled by gravity. That's why the ultimate bowler's prayer is: "God, please give me the strength to roll it easy!"

Toward that objective, as you assume the address position, take a very deep breath. Then exhale slowly. This will relax your body.

MISTAKE 100

Forgetting to Drop by the Bahr

During the last seconds of the San Francisco 49ers–New York Giants play-off game of 1990 with the Giants trailing 13–12, their field goal kicker, Matt Bahr, trotted onto the field for a long attempt. The game would determine which team would advance to Super Bowl XXV and which team's season would end.

Matt knew that he couldn't guarantee he'd split the uprights. So he decided that if he failed it would be a "happy miss" in which he struck the ball firmly. He could live with failure as long as that failure wasn't due to being tentative. His kick was good and his team went on to win the Super Bowl.

I fully endorse Matt's philosophy. When you need that one big shot to win a match, be certain that you are aggressive. It's perfectly permissible to miss (after all, every one of the greatest bowlers in history has occasionally fallen short in the clutch). Don't focus on the importance of the shot or the result. Instead, concentrate on just trying to make the best shot you can.

MISTAKE 101

Being a Cheese, Not the Ham

To be successful in the pros requires being able to perform well under the hot television lights when millions of viewers are watching and big money rides on every shot. Even the once-a-week amateur feels pressure sometimes.

Remember, you do absolutely nothing differently to strike in a so-called pressure situation than you do to strike during warm-ups. The analogy that I like to draw is to the circus star who walks the high wire.

The balance that's required to perform that task isn't unique to that individual. Some of us would have no trouble walking on a wire if that wire was but a few feet off the ground. But put that wire 50 feet in the air, and almost every one of us would start to contemplate the consequences of failure. Instead of looking at the wire, we'd see the ground below. And we'd freeze.

There are only two choices if you wish to be successful—either you enjoy center stage, or, at least, you're able to accept being there as the price that you pay for competing.

The pros who fare the best in televised championship-round competition tend to be the ones who look forward to that experience. Some of those are bona fide stars, such as Mike Aulby, Pete Weber, Don Johnson, and Dick Ritger. However, the top 10 win–loss percentage leaders include several good players who aren't superstars such as Danny Wiseman, Jim Pencak, and Randy Pedersen.

In contrast, some of the greatest bowlers in PBA history, led by Mark Roth and Earl Anthony, lost more games than they won in televised championship-round play. There are many theories on this odd statistic.

What's the difference between practicing in an empty center and having to throw a strike to win tens of thousands of dollars on national television? Absolutely nothing!

Among them is that their opponents relish the opportunity to challenge the "king of the hill." Also, Earl and Mark were so talented that they often reached the top five on lane conditions that weren't conducive to their style, while their foes were almost always bowling on their favorite conditions.

Dick Weber insists that much of his success in title rounds was owed to "being a ham." He truly enjoys the spotlight. So does Ernie Schlegel. Wanting to have a capacity crowd and a national TV audience watching makes it far easier to perform.

Here's a tip regarding how to react the next time that you're facing a big shot. Remind yourself that pressure is the reward that you reap for having bowled well. After all, there wouldn't be any pressure if your opponent had already locked up the game. Since that's not the case, you must have done something right to retain the chance at victory. That's why you should look forward to the opportunity to put yourself to the test as a reward.

Remember, even if you should fail, the odds are still pretty good that the sun will still rise in the east tomorrow morning.

Summary

The more you progress as a bowler, the more important your mental attributes become. To emulate Mike Aulby or Walter Ray Williams, Jr., strengthen your mental game by employing the following points.

1. Have a positive outlook to obtain postive results. Being confident is worth as much as possessing a powerful release or using the right ball.
2. Treat your equipment with the care it deserves.
3. Take the time to physically prepare yourself to bowl by thoroughly warming up.
4. Analyze the lane conditions you face and give thought to your strategy.
5. Give 100 percent on every shot.
6. Focus on what you must do to be successful, not on the importance of an upcoming delivery.
7. Think, but not for too long!
8. Be relaxed before executing your shot.
9. Enjoy moments when a game or a tournament is on the line by viewing pressure as a reward rather than as a burden.

Correcting 10 Common Bowling Flaws

Problem	Cause	Correction
Early timing	Premature pushaway	Push and step simultaneously
Late timing	Late pushaway	Overcompensate by pushing ball just before moving foot
Losing ball during release	Thumb hole too big	Add tape to hole
	Early timing	Push and step together
Ball goes left of target	Backswing away from body	Pushaway slightly away from body
	Early hand turn	Project ring finger toward the target
Ball goes right of target	Ball behind back during backswing	Slightly alter pushaway toward the body's center
	Late timing	Overcompensate by pushing ball just before moving foot
Hanging in thumb hole	Thumb hole too tight	Remove tape, enlarge hole, or wrap thumb in tissue and insert into the hole
Ball hooks too much	Slow ball speed	Hold ball higher during address and accelerate footwork
	Playing wrong angle	Move feet and target away from the side of your bowling hand

Problem	Cause	Correction
Ball doesn't hook enough	Excessive ball speed	Hold the ball lower during the address and slow down footwork
	Playing wrong angle	Move feet and target toward the side of your bowling hand
Ball hits pins weakly	Thumb not exiting from the ball cleanly	Remove tape, don't fully insert thumb, or use "tissue trick"
	Excessive ball speed	Slow down feet, hold ball lower in address position
	Ball too light	Use heavier ball if you can control it or play outside line
	Improper follow-through inside of 90 degrees	Follow through toward the ceiling
Sticking at the foul line	Substance on bottom of the sliding shoe	Wear slip covers between frames over shoes or clean the shoe's surface
	Sliding on heel, not the ball, of the foot	Push the slide with the sliding toes from the top of the backswing

APPENDIX

101 Common Bowling Errors

Error	Mistake	Page
1	Not Having a Pre-Shot Routine	2
2	Not Checking Your Shoes for Foreign Substances	2
3	Removing the Ball from the Rack Incorrectly	4
4	Incorrect Address Position	5
5	Failing to Dry the Bowling Hand	7
6	Taking the Wrong Exit Due to a Poor Entrance	8
7	Only in Politics Is Being in the Middle an Advantage	8
8	Incorrect Foot Position	11
9	Failing to Focus on a Target	11
10	Failing to Execute a Strong Pushaway	12
11	Being out of Time	18
12	Believing It's Better Late than Never	19
13	Not Understanding the Components of Timing	19
14	Starting out of Sync	22
15	Poor Conversions	22
16	Swinging for the Fences	22
17	Being a Race-ist	23
18	Not Analyzing Every Shot	23
19	Poor Address Position	30
20	Pathetic Pushaway	32
21	High Backswing	33
22	What Goes up Must Come Down	34
23	Not Stepping on the Pedal	34
24	Not Following Through to the Target	36
25	A Thumb That Overstays Its Welcome	45

Error	Mistake	Page
26	Acting Naturally	46
27	Lack of Leverage	48
28	Squeezing the Fruit While Being Watched	50
29	Throwing Three-Quarter 100 Percent the Same	50
30	Always Taking Moses's Advice	54
31	Failing to Be Well Balanced	58
32	Staying Upright Too Long	58
33	Only Donuts and Bagels Should Have Holes	60
34	Poor Sliding Technique	61
35	Failing to Hold the Pose	62
36	The Wandering Syndrome	64
37	Rearing up at the Line	64
38	Bending from the Waist	65
39	Smelling Something Foul	66
40	Taking the Proverbial "Three-Hour Tour"	70
41	Not Moving from Side to Side	72
42	Being a Blockhead	73
43	Failing to Adjust Ball Speed	74
44	Changing Ball Speed with the Heave-Ho Method	75
45	Forgetting the Axiom About an Exception to Every Rule	76
46	Maintaining the Same Distance from the Foul Line	78
47	Always Targeting the Arrows	79
48	Failing to Alter Wrist Positions	79
49	Never Taking the Subtle Approach	80
50	Being Closed-Minded	81
51	Failing to Use Tape	87
52	Throwing a Shot When the Thumb Hole Is Snug	88
53	Neglecting to Take Advantage of Wrist Devices	89
54	Exercising False Economy When Buying Footwear	90
55	Neglecting Your Hand	92
56	Not Taking Advantage of Grips	93
57	Poor Ball Selection	94
58	Reluctance to Change	100
59	Failing to Stay Clean	100
60	Why Carry the Weight of the World on Your Shoulders?	102

Error	**Mistake**	**Page**
61	Not Being Ready to Flash a Blade	102
62	Too Much Power to the People	107
63	Not Realizing That Light Makes Might	111
64	Going up the Boards	111
65	Not Knowing the Formulas	112
66	Not Having a Back-Up Plan	114
67	Forgetting to Bring Your Key	115
68	Not Knowing How to Shoot off the Strike Line	116
69	Seeing Double	118
70	Failing to Work on Improving Your Game	121
71	Employing Your Math Skills	123
72	To Practice Long Is to Practice Wrong	123
73	Failing to Plan	124
74	Exceeding the Speed Limit	125
75	Going Kaput by Staying Put	125
76	Not Challenging Yourself with Inferior Equipment	127
77	Forgetting Huey Lewis's Advice	127
78	Not Learning How to Alter Your Landing Zone	129
79	Not Hitting Your Stride	129
80	Only Competing in Competition	130
81	Sparing the Details	130
82	Lack of Vision	131
83	Not Taking Care of Business	136
84	Neglecting to Check Equipment Prior to Usage	137
85	Failing to Prepare the Body for Physical Activity	137
86	Forgetting to Have a Plan of Attack	139
87	Not Being a Boy Scout	140
88	Being a Soloist	140
89	Neglecting Common Courtesy	142
90	Negative Self-Talk	142
91	Refusing to Seek Help	144
92	One Mistake per Customer	146
93	Not Giving 100 Percent on Every Shot, Part I	147
94	Not Giving 100 Percent on Every Shot, Part II	148
95	Being a Spectator	148

Error	Mistake	Page
96	Not Knowing the Score	150
97	Think Long, Thing Wrong	151
98	Not Exploiting the Power of Your Imagination	151
99	Being as Tight as the Proverbial Drum	152
100	Forgetting to Drop by the Bahr	152
101	Being a Cheese, Not the Ham	153

Index

References to photographs are in italic type.

ABC Masters Tournament, 12, 14
Address position, 5–6, *6*, 30
Aim-and-flame strategy, 73
Air blower, 7, *7*
Airway Alleys, 46
American Bowling Congress, 67, 95
Analyzing shots, 23, 151
Ankles, 61
Anthony, Earl, 18, 28, 42–43, 78, 100, 102, 106, *106*, 109, 126, 145, 153, 155
Armswing, 8–10, *9*, *15*, 25–37. *See also* Backswing
  definition of, 25
  gravity and, 25–30, *26*, 34
  muscled, 27, 29, 36
  straight, 25, *35*
Arnold, Ray, 98
Arrows, 11, 41, 71, 79, 112
Attitude, 135
Aulby, Mike, 14, 18, 143, *143*, 145, 153, 155

Back stress, 4
Back-up ball, 44–45, *44*, 47–48
Back-up plans, 114–15, 148
Backswing, *9*, 17, 18, 20. *See also* Armswing
  high, 22, 33–34
  shoulder-high, 22, *33*, 33–34
  zenith, 34
Bahr, Matt, 152–53
Bainbridge Colonial Lanes, 2–3, 83, 97
Balance, 48, 58, 153
Ball to loop, *9*

Ball-return apparatus, 5
Benoit, Bob, 76
Block, 68
Boards, 111–14, *114*, 117
Bohn, Parker III, 108, 149–50
Borden, Fred, 11
Bowling. *See also specific topics*
  courtesy, 142
  exceptions to rules, 76–78
  flaws, 156–57. *See also specific flaws*
  importance of coaching, viii
  speed of game, 125
  as team sport, 140–42, *141*
  what players have in common, 57
Bowling bags, 96, *96*, 102
Bowling ball
  aligning, 8–10
  ball-return apparatus, 5
  beveling, 102–3
  "cheater," 95
  cleaning, 100–1, 137
  Columbia White Dot, 98
  cradling, 6
  drillings, 109
  dropping the ball, 32, *32*
  Ebonite Gyro, 94
  efficiency of equipment, 19
  end-over-end, 54
  plastic, 95
  porous cover stock, 96
  removing from rack, 4–5, *5*
  resin, 95, 96
  rotation, *50*
  rubber, 68, 94

selection of, 94–99
spare, 96–98
speed, 70, 74–76, *75*
squeezing, 50, 152
switching, 99–100, 109
thumb hole, 88, *88*
urethane, 95, 105
weight of, 99, 111
weights for, 95
wiping, 12
Bowling shoes
buying, 90–91
checking for foreign substance, 2–4
Break point, 67, *81*
Breathing, 11, 152
Brooklyn hit, 118
Buckley, Roy, 17, 22, 33
Burbank, California, 46
Burton, Nelson, Jr., 63, 74

Carrydown, 69, 101
Chagrin Falls, Ohio, 2, 83
Clendenon, Donn, 144
Closed-mindedness, 81–82
Columbia 300 Open, 149
Competition, 130, 148
Conversions, 22, 131. *See also* Spares
Cook, Steve, 28, 33, 60, 93
Cork insert, 87, *87*
Creating area, 69–70
Cross-lane conversions, 131

Davis, Dave, 27, 28
Dickinson, Gary, 54
Distance from foul line, 78
Dots, 12, 111
Duke, Norm, 18, 25, 29, 53, 54, 78, 82, 145
Durbin, Mike, 1, 41. *See also specific topics*

Easter, Sarge, 54
Elbows, 36

Equipment, 69, 83–104, 127, 136–37. *See also specific items*
checklist, 137
efficiency of, 19
storing, 136
Exit, 8. *See also* Release
sequential, 45–46

Feet. *See also* Sliding foot
foot-hand relationship, 16, 18
footwork, *15*, 21, 111–12, *112*
position of, 11
"running," 21, 22, 23
toes, 81, *81*
Ferraro, Dave, 17, *17*
"Filling the hole," 59, *59*
Finger inserts, 94
Fingers
exiting, 45–46
injury, 5
insertion, 54
nonbowling, 53
placement, 51
position of, 80
Finishes, 57–66
"filling the hole," 59, *59*
holding pose, 62–64
"overfilling the hole," 60–61
posting the shot, 61
stride, 58
Firestone Tournament of Champions, vii
Flagship Open, 108
Flooring, 3, 91
"track condition," 40
Focus, 11–12
Follow-through, 36–37, *36*, 62, 63, *133*, *157*
Formulas, 112–14
Foul line, 12
crossing, 66
distance from foul line, 78
rearing up at, 64–65, *65*

Full-roller, 40–43, *41*, *42*
    carrying power, 42

Gable House Bowl, 147
Genalo, Don, 147
Gillette, Kevin, 100
Going up the boards, 73, *73*
Grip, 8, 41, 80
    conventional, 93, *93*
    fingertip, 93–94, *93*
    semi-fingertip, 94

Hands
    blisters, 92, *92*
    drying, 7–8, *7*, 92–93, *92*
    foot-hand relationship, 16, 18
    supporting, 29
    timing of hand rotation, 40
Harahan, Tim, 84, 85
Hardwick, Billy, 33, 41
Heavy roll, 45
Helling, Don, 41
Hoard, Leroy, 102
Holman, Marshall, 18, 55, 145
Hook, 44–45, *44*, 47–48, 68, 156–57
Hooper, Chris, 145
Hudson, Tommy, 14
Humidity, 91
Husted, Dave, 9, 10, *101*

Johnson, Don, 9, 10, 18, 54, 145,
    153
Johnson, Jim, 91
Jouglard, Lee, 12
Jowdy, John, 48

Key pin, 115
Knees, 11, 58, 65
Knife, 102–3

Lane. *See also* Oil
    conditions, 68–70, *68*
    dry versus wet, 67, 72–73

geography of, 71, 112
    inspecting, 70–71, 139–40
    lingo, 71
Laub, Larry, 84, 85, 88
Laying ball short, 129
Learn, Bob, Jr., 108, *108*, 109
Leverage, 48–49, *49*
Lift, 45–46
Lofting shots, *128*, 129
Lou, Alvin, 103

Marino, Hank, 44
Marshall, Jim, 147
Math skills, 123
Mazza, John, 108, 144, 145
Mecurio, Walter "Skang," 97
Mental game, 135–55
    anger, 146, 147
    attitude, 135
    equipment and, 136–37
    mental imaging, 151–52
    preparation, 140
    seeking help, 144–46
    self-talk, 142–44, 148
    warm-up, 137–39
Milutinovic, Bora, 146, 147
Mirrors, 131
Monacelli, Amleto, 33
Moore, C. K., 149, 150, *150*
"Mr. Average Builder," vii, 121

"Natural starting point," 78
Nelson, Burton, Jr., 61
Newton, Isaac, 25

Oil
    accumulation on ball, 1, 2
    migration on lane, 54
    oily versus dry lane, 67, 72
Older players, 111, *138*
"Out of bounds," 73
"Overfilling the hole," 60–61
Owen, Mickey, 147

Ozio, David, 25, 28, 60, 81–82, 82, 108, 123

Palombi, Ron, Jr., 53
Pappas, George, 84
PBA National Championship, 14, 17, 81
Pedersen, Randy, 108, 153
Pencak, Jim, 153
Petraglia, Johnny, 108
Physical adjustment
    altering positions of wrists, 79–80
    distance from foul line, 78
    strike line altering, 72–74, 76–78
Physical adjustments, 67–82
Pin bowling, 12
Pins, 115, 115
    visible, 71
Planning, 114–15, 124, 139–40, 148
Playing outside, 73, 73
Pocket, 64
Pocket split, 17
Polishing machine, 83–84
Pose, holding, 62–64, 62, 63
Posting the shot, 61
Practice, 121–34, 122, 154
    amount of time, 123–24
    from different angles, 125–27
    math skills, 123
    planning, 124
Pre-shot routine, 1–14
    address position, 5–6
    aligning the ball, 8–10
    ball preparation, 1–2, 4–5
    exit, 8
    focusing on target, 11–12
    hands, 7–8
    shoes, 2–4
Pritts, Jimmie, Jr., 147
Professional Bowlers Association
    National Tour, vii
    Rookie of the Year, vii
Pushaways, 12–14, 13, 27, 31, 32–33
    dropping the ball, 32, 32

high, 32, 32
imaginary table, 12, 20, 20, 21, 29, 32
upward, 14

Release, 8, 20, 27, 36–37, 39–55
    back-up ball, 44–45, 44, 47–48
    "driver," 53
    full-roller, 40–43
    losing ball, 156
    semi-roller, 39–40, 39, 47
    spinner, 43–44, 43, 55
    straight, 50–52, 51
    three-quarter, 50–54, 50
    women bowlers, 46–48
Resin bag, 7, 7, 93
Reverse block, 73
Reverse hook. See Back-up ball
Rhythm, 15
Richard, Ed, 149
Ritger, Dick, 63, 145, 153
Roth, Mark, 18, 43, 53, 103, 106, 145, 153, 155

Salvino, Carmen, 62, 63
"Sand traps," 3
Schlegel, Ernie, 17, 155
Score, 147, 150–51
Seaver, Tom, 144
Self-talk, 142–44, 148
Semi-roller, 39–40, 39, 47
Semiz, Teata, 84
Short slide, 65
Shoulders, 9, 9, 102
    dropped, 132
    squaring, 127
Skid-roll-hook sequence, 68
Sliding foot, 6, 6, 48, 49, 61, 117
Smith, Keith "Doc," 97
Snead, Sam, 67
Spare shooter, 130–31, 131
Spares, 105–19
    double wood, 107–11, 118
    footwork, 111–12

formulas, 112–14
non-double wood, 107–11
strike line and, 116–18
Spectators, 148–50
Speed, 70, 74–76, 75, 125
Spinner, 43–44, 43, 55
Splits, 105–19
    baby, 116
    formulas, 112–14
    "Greek church split," 147
Sport psychologists, 145
Stefanich, Jim, 10, 10, 108
Sticking at the line, 2–4, 157
Stretching routines, 137–39, 138
Stride, 58, 129
Strike line, 116–18
    altering, 72–74
Stus, Gene, 65
Sullins, Harry, 17
Swingout, 9, 10, 10
Synchronized stroking, 11
Syracuse Open, 103

Tampa Sertoma Open, 41
Tapp, Charlie, 109, 110
Target, 11–12, 36–37, 64, 79, 156
    dropping the curtain, 64
    timing and, 20
Taylor, Bill, 42
Texas Highland Lanes, 149
Three-quarter release, 50–54, 50
Thumb
    exiting, 8, 36, 41, 45–46, 80–81, 157
    position of, 80–81
    size, 87
    thumb hole, 88, 88, 156
Thumb-hole tape, 86, 87–88
Timing, 15–24
    components of, 19–21
    definition of, 15, 16, 17
    of hand rotation, 40

late versus early, 16–17, 16, 18–19, 21, 156
Toes, 81, 81
Torrance, California, 147
Tournament of Champions, 14
Traber, Dave, 149
"Track condition," 40
Track shot, 41
Triple Crown, 17
Two-spray system, 101

U.S. National Team, 146
U.S. Open, 14, 17

Videotaping, 132
Vision, 131–34

Waist, bending, 65–66, 66
Warm-up, 137–39, 138
Warren, Del, 60
Webb, Wayne, 12, 44
Weber, Dick, 18, 25, 28, 28, 106, 145, 155
Weber, Pete, 17, 18, 22, 33, 145, 153
Welu, Billy, 54
Williams, Ted, 57
Williams, Walter Ray, Jr., 9, 10, 18, 28–29, 36, 53, 54, 78, 106, 143, 145, 145, 146, 155
Wise, Bernie, 84
Wiseman, Danny, 153
Women bowlers, 46–48
World Cup, 146
Wrist
    altering positions, 79–80
    angle, 52, 52
    cupping, 52–53
    stress, 4
Wrist devices, 89–90, 89, 111

Youngstown Open, 41